Education, Conservatism, and the Rise of a Pedagogical Elite in Colombian Panama

Rolando de la Guardia Wald

Education, Conservatism, and the Rise of a Pedagogical Elite in Colombian Panama

1878–1903

palgrave
macmillan

Rolando de la Guardia Wald
University of Panama
Panama City, Panama

ISBN 978-3-030-50045-0   ISBN 978-3-030-50046-7   (eBook)
https://doi.org/10.1007/978-3-030-50046-7

This Palgrave Macmillan imprint is published by the registered company Springer Nature Switzerland AG.
The registered company address is: Gewerbestrasse 11, 6330 Cham, Switzerland

ACKNOWLEDGEMENTS

During the long process of writing my doctoral dissertation and this book, I received priceless help from many people and institutions. Ms Linda Braus and Ms Milana Vernikova and the whole team at Palgrave Macmillan have been more than understanding during the process of writing my first book. I owe them the time and effort I used to fulfil this goal. Also, I would like to thank Panama's Secretaría Nacional de Ciencia, Tecnología e Innovación (National Secretary for Science, Technology and Innovation) for financing my doctoral studies at University College London.

My gratitude also goes to the academic and administrative staff in the Department of History at University College London. Studying there was an exciting intellectual journey. I will always be indebted to my main supervisor Professor Nicola Miller and second supervisor Doctor Christopher Abel for their advice and infinite patience during and after the writing of my thesis. While broadening my research, I received the inestimable mentorship of Professor Eduardo Posada-Carbó at the Latin American Centre (LAC) of the University of Oxford. I cannot leave out all the scholars who stimulated my intellect at the History Department, the Faculty of Education and especially at the Centre for the History of Women's Education at the University of Winchester, in particular to Stephanie Spencer, Joyce Goodmand and Sue Anderson. This book would not exist had not the following professors encouraged me to study history and education and given me precious guidance since I was an undergraduate student: Dr Iván Jaksic, Dr Alfredo Figueroa Navarro, Dr Carlos Guevara-Mann, Dr Javier Laviña, Dr Gabriella dalla Corte (Rest in Peace),

and Dr Roberto Arosemena (Rest in Peace), Dr Etilvia Arjona (Rest in Peace).
I must recognise all the support received from the authorities of the University of Panama: Dr Eduardo Flores, Dr José Emilio Moreno, Dr Jaime Gutiérrez, Dr Olmedo García. Just as crucial has been the guidance of Dr Celestino Araúz, Dr Patricia Pizzurno, Dr Fermina Santana, Dr Yolanda Marco and Professor Fernando Aparicio. I have also to recognise the assistance of the Biblioteca Nacional de Panamá, the Biblioteca Nacional de Colombia and Biblioteca Luis Ángel Arango, and the Hispanic Division at the Library of Congress. At Florida State University-Panama, Dr Alexandra Anyfanti was a beacon of support. Finally, but not least, I appreciate the support received from the President of the Panama Canal Museum, Hildegard Vásquez and its staff.

Through the years, I have shared intellectually nurturing ideas with colleagues and friends: Dr Michela Coletta, Dr Guido Van Meersbergen, Diana Zárate, Dr Edgar García, Dr Hana Qugana, Dr Katherine Quinn, Dr Katherine Marino, Dr Carlos Brando, Dr Meritxell Simon-Martin, Dr Michael Conniff, Dr Andrea Rosen, Dr Miroslaw Bem, Carlos Solís, Dr Mariana León, Magister Andrea Miranda, and Lauren De'Ath.

Finally, the most important source of motivation has been my family's unconditional love. I dedicate this work to them: Rolando de la Guardia González, Helen Wald de de la Guardia, Alexandra de la Guardia, Georgeana de la Guardia, Ana Lucía Calderón, Ignacio Calderón, Alastair Forrest, Archer Forrest, Eloise Forrest and Ryan Forrest.

CONTENTS

1   Introduction   1

2   *La Regeneración* and *Paz Científica* in Colombian
    Panama, 1878–1903   41

3   *La Regeneración* and the Rise of the Pedagogical Elite in
    Panama, 1878–1903   91

4   Conclusion   139

Annex 1   147

Annex 2   151

Annex 3   155

Annex 4   159

Annex 5   163

Index   171

CHAPTER 1

Introduction

After the consecration of Panama's final secession from Colombia in 1903, Isthmian statesmen, politicians, intellectuals and men of letters began to envision a future of peace and progress. In their imagination, this almost tangible promise of modernity was far away from those past experiences of political turbulence that chained the Isthmus to Colombia's destiny and that dragged them down together towards regression, stagnation and fratricide. A visualisation of that future was represented by conservative poet and satirical fabulist Rodolfo Caicedo (1868–1905) in 'Paz y Progreso' ('Peace and Progress').

The poet exalted the bravery of 'paladin' Estaban Huertas (1876–1943), the Colombian military man who aided the Panamanian independentists in the events of 1903. Caicedo said that he did not want to remember his 'deeds as a warrior … in these peaceful hours'. Instead, he wanted to forget the violent past and celebrate Huerta's 'delirium of liberty that made his heart rebel' and guided Manuel Amador Guerrero, the leader of the Independence movement and first constitutional President of Panama, to 'strike a blow on the iron lace' that united Panama to Colombia, a metaphor symbolising a forceful yet peaceful 'victory'.

The poem, however, dedicated more stanzas to Caicedo's vision of the present–future or 'horizon of expectations'. His verses began by praising the peaceful character of Panama's Independence, a 'victory without tears

© The Author(s) 2020
R. de la Guardia Wald, *Education, Conservatism, and the Rise of a Pedagogical Elite in Colombian Panama*,
https://doi.org/10.1007/978-3-030-50046-7_1

and mourning' that 'garners a fervourous applause from the universe'. Panama's present-future was that of being home to the 'white flag'. Then 'Paz y Progreso' recited:

How beautiful is Peace! She has
posed a strong wall to Nemesis.
She has come to save us from an abyss ...

Progress will come under her protection ...
The Isthmus [will be] opened by a deep wound
[and this] ditch will be a brilliant lighthouse
And a fountain of life.

Those who suffer the miseries of a beggar
Will come as a noisy beehive
To look for bread and beg for coating.

And they will get it! ...

Now that the deadly strife ended ...
[sleeping] under the same roof
[are] those who fought on opposing sides

... at their unripe early years
Simple and happy young men will not go,
... to build stairs
For astute caudillos to climb.

They will not go to kill each other with hatred,
So that, at the end of the furious combat,
their juvenile blood serves as fertiliser
Of the infamous battlefield of ambition.

Now replacing the horrible stampeding sound
Of the formidable and terrifying cannon,
There is the cheerful noise of workshops
And the precious buzzing of schools.

The light of divine instruction will go
From the palace to the humble hut
Restoring the ruins of morality ...

And smoke from factories that rises
like incense to the infinite dome
Will replace the blackened cloud
That rose from cursed gunpowder.

A human being will be made of the indigenous who moans
… in the sour obscurantism,
… that oppress his soul …
Without him even knowing

And due to hunger, the flower of innocence
Will not go withering to adorn brothels …

… in our unrivalled, fertile soil,
There is a promise of a copious banquet
That will be [more than] enough the nurture the world.[1]

Rodolfo Caicedo's poem was written in January of 1904. It depicts the horizon of expectations of a new nation-state. The poet drives the reader into a juxtaposing flow: he emphasises the need for abandoning and forgetting the warrior-like past, yet he constantly restores images that remember the horrors of war. With this he reminds his readers that peace had saved Isthmians from crisis and certain decadence, but simultaneously compelled them to envision that the new present had placed Panama just at the edge of modernity.

Peace imposed on Panama the destiny to be generous with the world, so that the 'deep wound' caused by the construction of the Panama Canal would provide for Isthmians and foreigners alike. The new situation would lead to tolerance between those who 'fought on opposing sides', under the influx of 'Nemesis', the Greek goddess of divine retribution and revenge but re-imagined by Caicedo as a goddess of human discord. Now they will sleep under the roof of a fraternal Panama. The sounds and smoke of war will dissipate and young men will not go into battle to die unnecessarily. Caicedo predicted that factories will bring advancements in science and technology and, more importantly, productive work. The rise of incense-smelling smoke from factories to an 'infinite dome' is also a sign of spiritual elevation. The smoke produced by hard work and peacefulness permits Isthmians to approximate Heaven. Yet, just as essential to progress was instruction. Under this new peace, workshops and schools will emit 'cheerful noise' and a 'precious buzzing'. These are images of happiness, and, in the particular case of schools, of innocence. All this invokes the sensation that a 'divine instruction' or moral and religious education will transform schools and workshops into vessels for moral purification, which

---

[1] Rodolfo Caicedo. 'Paz y Progreso (1904)', *Revista Lotería* N° 60 (Panamá: Mayo de 1946), pp. 16–19.

was imperative for the process of regenerating Panama. Using a conde-
scending tone, Caicedo assured that even the indigenous peoples, who
lived in abandonment and ignorance, will be enlightened and learn about
the reasons of their suffering. To the eyes of the poet they will become
civilised. Finally, this new era of high morality and wealth will prevent
young girls from becoming prostitutes.

The poem reflects that Isthmian independentists had conceptualised
the era of union to Colombia as a period of material and moral deterioration. They confidently projected the image that by declaring independence, the Republic of Panama had already made the right adjustments
to truly transform into a modern nation. Thus, a new yet familiar horizon of expectations opened to many Isthmians. It was new because a
recently created small-state, the Republic of Panama, and its leaders did
not require to negotiate their local designs with peers from distant areas
of Colombia; whether it was advantageous or not, now they could deal
with great world powers on their own. The new sensation of freedom
and hope for a better future exemplified by the construction of the
Canal engendered an innovative prediction in which Panama would
represent the epitome of cosmopolitanism.

Despite the fact that the situation of permanent independence was new
and represented a point of no return, the expectations portrayed in 'Paz y
Progreso' were still familiar to Panamanians. Caicedo's poetry was clearly
imbued with the discourse of the political reform called *La Regeneración*.
The philosophy of this reform marked Isthmian intellectual and political life
from 1878 to at least 1903.[2] This process was conducted by the
joint Government of partisans of the Conservative Party and members of
the moderate faction of the Liberal Party or *Liberales Independientes*.
The alliance between these previous rivals was possible because of political
pragmatism and convenience. But, additionally, there was a process of doc-
trinal transformation of both liberalism and conservatism in Colombia and
Panama as intellectuals and politicians on each side of the spectrum modified their traditional dogmas. Since moderate liberals perceived excessive
liberalism in the political practices of their co-partisans, the *Liberales
Radicales*, they sought to control the effects of those policies through the
application of positivist premises to governance. On their part, some
Conservatives attempted to reconcile religion with new developments
in science. Elaborating from positivist and Christian notions of reasonability

---

[2] David Bushnell. *The Making of Modern Colombia. A nation in spite itself* (Berkeley, Los
Angeles, London: University of California Press, 1993), pp. 140–154.

or 'cosmopolitanism', *Liberales Independientes* and Conservatives orchestrated a political project that called for regeneration as the path to attain
'scientific peace', order and progress. The horizon of expectations that
Caicedo portrayed in his poem was, after all, the same as those of his peers
from Colombia and Panama before 1903, but artistically it was presented as
new. In spite of this illusion of novelty, all of the above implies that the early
philosophical and political foundations of the new Republic of Panama are
not to be found only in liberalism, but on the precepts of the regeneration
conceived by conservatised-liberals and conservatives and that derived from
the ideas of personages so loathed in conventional Panamanian historiography such as Rafael Núñez and Miguel Antonio Caro.

With this in mind, this book questions the claim that Panamanian
proto-nationalism and nationalism and the construction of the Panamanian
national state was overwhelmingly dominated by an urban and 'commercial bourgeoisie' who adhered dogmatically to the principles of classic liberalism. In addition, it makes a point to extricate itself from the
historiography that presents Panama as a product of the construction of
the Canal and Panamanian identity as fabrication of or a reaction to United
States' imperialism. Instead, it emphasises the input of conservatives and
the conservative-leaning liberals in Colombian state-making. Furthermore,
it illustrates that many Panamanian leaders had concerns that extended
beyond exploiting the Isthmus's geography for the sake of obtaining commercial benefits. They also dealt with intellectual, moral, social and cultural issues. Through the lenses of utilitarian, positivist or conservative
mind frames, Isthmian intellectuals debated about topics such as religion,
morality and civism; the proper use of Spanish language; the use and usefulness of science and technology; law, rights and duties; trade and indus-
try; consumerism and materialism; and education and instruction.

Because education policy was a key tool in the reproduction and dissemination of conservative and positivist-liberal views and to perpetuate a
model that would lead to the supposed 'salvation' and modernisation of
Colombian and Panamanian societies, it was directed to prepare a group
of elite educators via the creation of teachers' schools or *escuelas normales*.
The members of this pedagogical elite were active agents in the spread of
Catholic and positivist understandings of reason and science. That is, these
new professional educators not only taught technical skills and modern
scientific knowledge, but also what they considered proper moral social
behaviour and etiquette from the perspective of Catholicism and their
"scientific" study of society.

HISTORICAL CONTEXT: LATE NINETEENTH-CENTURY COLOMBIAN PANAMA, 1878–1903

For the case of Panama, this book marks the beginning of *La Regeneración* in 1878, and locates its end at the moment of the Independence of Panama from Colombia in 1903.

By 1903, Colombia and therefore Panama had experienced several civil wars; only in the last quarter of the nineteenth century, there were armed conflicts in 1875, 1876–1877, 1885, 1895, and 1899–1902. The last was the famously violent War of the Thousand Days. Adding to the national turmoil, the fact that the federalist political system established by the Colombian Constitution of 1863 did not allow the central government to intervene in the internal affairs of the *estado soberanos* (sovereign states) of the *Estados Unidos de Colombia* (United States of Colombia) resulted in constant revolts and coups in various states, including Panama. In 1875, the Liberal Party fragmented into the dominant *Liberales Radicales* (Radical Liberals) and the moderate *Liberales Independientes* (Independent Liberals) led by Rafael Núñez (1825–1894), a politician and intellectual from Cartagena. Observing the causes and consequences of the civil war of 1876–1877, Núñez took the opportunity of giving an inaugural speech during the investiture of President Julián Trujillo in 1878, and posited that there was an urgent need for political reform in Colombia. He affirmed that the country had to either 'confront fundamental administrative regeneration or catastrophe'.[3] The result of such reform would be that '[instead] of that kind of sterile and submissive peace that sometimes bayonets impose, we will have a fertile peace'.[4] This speech represented a state of purposes or a manifesto of *La Regeneración*.

Núñez was heavily influenced by positivist ideas, especially those of John Stuart Mill and Herbert Spencer. He was exposed to them when exercising the post of consul of Colombia at Liverpool between 1864 and 1875. Before, and especially while he occupied the presidency (1880–1882, 1884–1886, 1886–1892 and 1892–1894), he designed policies that, supposedly, took positivism into praxis. Núñez sustained that his own analysis of political experiences demonstrated that order,

---

[3] Rafael Núñez. 'Rejeneración administrativa fundamental o catástrofe'. Cruz Cárdenas, Antonio, ed. *Grandes oradores colombianos.* (Bogotá: Imprenta Nacional de Colombia, 1997), p. 3. http://www.banrepcultural.org/blaavirtual/indice
[4] Ibid, p. 4.

peace and progress could only be achieved in Colombia if the political system was centralised and the executive empowered. Because this conclusion was conceived "scientifically", he named its future result '*Paz Científica*' or Scientific Peace.

Arguing that leniency with the opposition was necessary to reach and maintain order and peace,[5] Núñez made political concessions to the Conservatives.[6] In 1885, this led to another civil war, in which the *Liberales Independientes* allied with the Conservatives against the *Liberales Radicales*. The latter were defeated, and a year later, Núñez's government promulgated the new Constitution of 1886. This signified the consolidation of *La Regeneración*. The alliance between conservatives and moderate liberals became even more palpable when they founded the *Partido Nacional* (National Party) in 1886.

The new foundational code of law was heavily influenced by the input of Conservative leader Miguel Antonio Caro (1843–1909), who became Vice-President (1886–1892 and 1892–1894) and, President of Colombia (1894–1898) after the death of Núñez. Another key figure in this constituting process was the former Bishop of Panama (1875–1884) and Archbishop of Colombia (1884–1899), José Telésforo Paúl (1831–1889). The Constitution of 1886 contained clauses that aimed at centralising the government by giving more power to the executive, reinforcing their control over freedom of the press,[7] increasing the penalties for different kind of crimes (including the instauration of the death penalty),[8] or limiting the autonomy of the different *departamentos* by having the President name the governors.[9] In addition, all citizens could vote for members to the Municipal Council and the Departmental Assembly,[10] but suffrage for selecting *Electores* (who then voted for the President) was limited by income controls, literacy levels and property ownership.[11] For Isthmian federalists and even some conservatives, one of the

---

[5] Rafael Núñez. 'La Paz Científica', *La Reforma Política en Colombia*. (Bogotá: no publisher indicated, 1888), pp. 94–97.

[6] Gerardo Molina. *Las Ideas Liberales en Colombia–1849–1914*. 4ta. Edición. (Bogotá: Ediciones Tercer Mundo, 1974), pp. 131–156.

[7] Articles 42 and K. *Constitución de la República de Colombia de 1886*. Edición Oficial (Bogotá: Imprenta de Vapor de Zalamea HS., 1886), pp. 13 and 57.

[8] Article 29, Ibid., p. 10.

[9] Article 120, Ibid., pp. 32–34.

[10] Articles 172, Ibid., p. 46.

[11] Article 173, Ibid.

most problematic aspects of the Constitution of 1886 was the stipulation that Panama would be ruled from the executive in Bogotá through 'special laws'.[12] This Article was somewhat modified by a new decree in 1892, however.[13] Lastly, the government stimulated nationalism based on Hispanic traditionalism and culture. Thus, the constitution declared Catholicism the religion 'of the nation' but it was not official and remained independent from the state.[14] Moreover, it allowed the return of religious education and priests into schools.[15]

It is important to highlight that this friendly approximation to the Catholic Church was enhanced through the signing of two concordats with the Vatican in 1887 and 1892. In sum, the new constitution facilitated a return of conservative influence on political power and led to a period known as the 'conservative hegemony' which ran from 1886 to 1930.[16]

Although the *Liberales Radicales* did not present a candidate for the electoral campaign of 1892, the competition caused divisions among conservatives. They split between the *Conservadores Nacionales* (National Conservatives) and the *Conservadores Históricos* (Historical Conservatives). The former supported the existing *Liberal Independiente*–Conservative alliance under the platform of the *Partido Nacional* and the selection of Caro as candidate for the Vice-Presidency; the latter claimed that they preserved original and true conservative doctrines by rejecting cooperation with liberals, and, therefore, chose General Marcelino Vélez as presidential candidate. Others promoted the presidential candidacy of a third conservative politician, José Domingo Ospina. The victors were Núñez and Caro. By 1894, the rift between Conservatives went further after Núñez died and Caro took office. This was followed by the civil war of 1895. The *Liberales Radicales* wrongly calculated that they could take advantage of the diatribe, but they were defeated. The elections of 1898 exacerbated the confrontation between Conservatives to the point that Caro opted not to run

---

[12] Article 201, Ibid., p. 52.

[13] Ministerio de Instrucción Pública de Colombia. *Informe que el Ministro de Instrucción Pública presenta al Congres de Colomba en sus sesiones ordinaria de 1894.* (Bogotá: Imprenta de la Luz, 1894), p. LI.

[14] Article 38, Ibid., p. 12.

[15] Articles 41 and 54, Ibid., pp. 13 and 16.

[16] Eduardo Posada-Carbó. 'Limits of Power: Elections under the Conservative Hegemony in Colombia, 1886–1930', *The Hispanic American Historical Review*, Vol. 77, N° 2 (Durham: Duke University Press, 1997), pp. 245; Molina, pp. 142–143.

for president. Instead, he attempted to conciliate both conservative factions by backing up the presidential campaign in favour of Manuel Antonio Sanclemente, an adept of the *Conservadores Nacionales*, and for the Vice-Presidency of José María Marroquín, a *Conservador Histórico*. Although the electoral formula won, Caro's plans went in the other direction when Sanclemente got sick and left his governmental position. Caro urged him to retake the presidency, which he did, but, in 1900, Marroquín orchestrated an internal coup and established himself as president. Almost simultaneously, the *Liberales Radicales* made the same miscalculation as in 1895 and revolted in 1899. This was the beginning of the War of the Thousand Days (1899–1902). Again, the *Liberales Independientes* and both factions of the Conservative Party remained allied. The armed conflict ended in a victory for the government. In Panama the War of the Thousand Days lasted longer, but when the governmental forces were ready to quell the revolt in the Isthmus, the belligerents signed a peace treaty on U.S.S. Wisconsin in 1902. The same year, the Congress of Colombia signed the Herran–Hay Treaty with the United States regarding the construction of a canal through Panama. Nevertheless, the Colombian legislative decided not to ratify it, a decision that catalysed the Independence of Panama in 3 November 1903, an action that required the collaboration of the United States. This permanent secession, however, was disapproved by many Panamanians, such as *Liberal Radical* Belisario Porras, moderate Liberal Pablo Arosemena, and Conservative Juan B. Pérez y Soto.[17]

Regarding public instruction, in the 1870s, the Colombian government made new efforts to professionalise education by hiring German experts in pedagogics and school organisation and by founding *escuelas normales* or teachers' schools. Thus, Oswald Wirsing was sent to Panama and became the first director of the All-Men Teachers School or *Escuela Normal de Varones*. However, the most famous figure in the development of education in nineteenth century Panama was Manuel José Hurtado. According to his biographers, he was a key in the establishing of the *Dirección de Instrucción Pública* (Directorate of Public Instruction) in 1870.[18] This Directorate was an institution in charge of making policy to design the goals, expand the outreach, and evaluate the quality of

---

[17] All these events coincided with the arrival and demise of the French-led construction of a canal (1878–1903) and the arrival of large numbers of immigrants. Despite its relevance, it was not viable to study the topic in this book.

[18] José Antonio Susto and Simón Eliet Simón. *La Vida y Obra de Manuel José Hurtado*. (Panamá: Talleres Gráficos, 1921), p. 53.

education.[19] Hurtado was, in fact, *Director* from 1872 to 1879.[20] Under his directorship, the previously mentioned *Escuela Normal de Varones* was founded. In 1878, he persuaded the Governor of Panama, Buenaventura Correoso, to found an *Escuela Normal de Institutoras* (All-Girls Teachers School).[21] Seemingly, his commitment to promote public instruction, and, especially, the training of future teachers went beyond mere administrative work. For example, he covered the expenses of the *Escuela Normal de Varones* out of his own pocket, so it could remain open during the civil war of 1876.[22] In order to recognise this, as early as 1879, the Government of the State of Panama issued a law ordering that a portrait of Manuel José Hurtado should be displayed in all schools of the Isthmus.[23] In spite of these accolades, Hurtado decided to resign due to some disagreements with the Governor and retired a year after his portrait law was issued.[24]

Under his directorship, the *Escuela Normal de Varones* graduated some of the most important conservative and moderate liberal teachers of the next generation: Nicolás Pacheco, Mélchor Lasso de la Vega and Nicolás Victoria Jaén.

After the Civil War of 1885, many schools closed, including the *Escuela Normal de Varones*. However, the situation apparently improved as the number of schools gradually increased. Amongst the most important schools founded during *La Regeneración* there was the Colegio Balboa. It was created in 1888 with the purpose of consolidating secondary schooling in Panama and of harmonising Isthmian education with that of the rest of Colombia by imitating the curriculum of the Colegio del Rosario, the most prestigious teaching establishment in Bogotá. As indicated, during *La Regeneración*, priests and nuns from different orders governed many public schools, due to the Constitutions of 1886 and the ratification of the Concordats of 1887 and 1892. For instance, the order of Saint Vincent de Paúl ruled *Escuela de Señoritas* in the neighbourhood of Santa Ana in the *Arrabal*[25] and the *Seminario Menor* (Lower Seminary) in Santiago de

---

[19] Ibid., p 44.
[20] Ibid., p. 49.
[21] Ibid., p 57.
[22] Ibid., p. 54.
[23] Ibid., p. 58.
[24] Ibid., p. 57.
[25] José Agustín Torres, Inspector General de Instrucción Pública del Departamento de Panama. *Informe que el Ministro de Instrucción Pública presenta al Congreso de Colombia en sus sesiones de 1890.* (Bogotá: Imprenta de 'La Luz', 1890), p. 135.

Veraguas.[26] In 1892, the Colegio de Balboa was placed under the admin-
istration of *Reverendos Padres Escolapios* (or the Order of Calasanz), which
implies that a highly organised body stepped in to reinforce Catholic education in Panama City.[27]

Coinciding with this, in 1893, Ricardo Arango, a commerce graduate
from Fort Edward, became the first Isthmian governor of Panama since the
promulgation of the Constitution of 1886.[28] According to some sources,
Panamanian public instruction was deplorable until he took office[29] (See
Annex 1). Although Arango died in office in 1898, it was during his gover-
norship, and mainly through the agency of his Secretary of Public Instruction,
lawyer Salomón Ponce Aguilera, that the conservative and moderate liberal pedagogical elite truly rose to direct or teach at prominent schools and
occupy positions in the local Secretariat of Public Instruction.

LITERATURE REVIEW

In spite of the fact that the inhabitants of the Isthmus of Panama lived under
a government formed by Conservatives and *Liberales Independientes* from
1878 until 1903, few works explore their influence in the development of
Isthmian identities, and the formation of the Panamanian state. In most his-
toriographies, these different political factions are generally put together
under the single label of 'conservatives'. This is a historiographic tradition
that presents the dynamics of Isthmian political and intellectual life as a simple story of liberals clashing against conservatives. Subsequently, there is a
lack of knowledge about the potential and complex amalgamations and
negotiations between various forms of conservatism. For decades, the

[26] 'Informe de Baldomendo Carles, Rector del Seminario de Panama', Ibid., p. 298.
[27] *Informe que el Ministro de Instrucción Pública Presenten al Congreso de Colombia en sus sesiones de 1894.* (Bogotá: Imprenta de la Luz, 1894), p. XXVIII.
[28] Frank Safford indicates that Arango studied engineering. He might have confused Arango with his son Ricardo Arango Jr. There are other cases of Panamanians who studied for technical careers. Frank Safford mentioned Demetrio Blas Arosemena, Blas Paredes and Francisco Fábrega, but there is little information about them and they did not occupy important political positions between 1878 and 1903. Safford, *Ideal of the Practical. Colombia's Struggle to Form a Technical Elite.* (Austin and London: University of Texas Press, 1976), Appendix 2, p. 261
[29] Octavio Méndez Pereira. *Historia de la instrucción pública en Panamá.* (Panamá, Editorial La Moderna, 1916), p. 16; Juan Bosco Bernal. 'La Educación en Panamá: antecedentes, tendencias y perspectivas', *Panamá: Cien Años de República.* (Panamá: Manfer, S.A., 2004), p. 53.

hegemonic Panamanian scholarship has stressed the importance of certain forms of liberalism (especially *radicalismo* or the utilitarianism of the *Liberales Radicales*) in the shaping of Panamanian identities; therefore, a revision of the political, intellectual and ideological impact of different conservative factions and the *Liberales Independientes* is thus long overdue. The purpose of this work, though, is not to present an apologetic narrative of conservatism, but to render a more comprehensive understanding of the development of Panamanian proto-national and national identities.

Teleologies of 'Transitism', 'Hanseatism' and Liberal Nationalism

Based on the connection between liberalism defence of free trade and the supposed wish of Isthmian elites to transform their country into a 'commercial emporium', some of the most influential texts about the history of Panamanian identity conclude that liberal thinkers and politicians had an overwhelming force in Panama from 1826 to at least the 1920s. In these narratives, a generalised hyper-consciousness about the importance of the Isthmus's geographical position and its economic potential appear as factors that have perpetuated a liberal mentality inherent to Panamanian idiosyncrasy. Although some of this historiography had vindicated the important role of subaltern, poor and ethnically-racially-mixed population, especially that of the outskirts of Panama City or *Arrabal*, they still preserve the dominant narrative by projecting liberal values into the mindframe of the nonprivileged majorities as a whole. These stories have constructed an 'official history' and a teleology of liberalism.[30]

Thus, this conventional national history tends to centre on a description of documents, events and people selected as relevant to illustrate the particularities of the nation and its alleged attachment to liberalism. For instance, the documents and movements that led to the secessions of Panama from Colombia of 1830, 1831 and 1840–1841 appear as highly nationalist and anti-Colombian, and inspired by strong liberal beliefs. Liberal lawyers, intellectuals and politicians, such as Justo Arosemena (the 'father of Panamanian nationality') or Buenaventura Correoso, are, respectively, presented as national heroes or described as representatives of most of the poor majorities of the *Arrabal*.

---

[30] Reymundo Gurdián Guerra. 'Entre luces y sombras: La enseñanza de las "Historia de Panamá" y la Historiografía Republicana.' in *Historia General de Panamá*. Vol. III. Tomo II. Capítulo XVIII. Alfredo Castillero Calvo (ed.) (Panamá: Comité del Centenario de la República, 2004), 185.

A very important group of works have revised the traditional nationalist historiography and questioned the histories of high-minded and heroic members of the Panamanian political elites by attributing to them a more mundane character. In this line, some of the most influential are the articles and books written in the 1960s and 1970s by Ricaurte Soler,[31] Alfredo Castillero Calvo,[32] and Alfredo Figueroa Navarro.[33] These analyses have a structuralist, Marxist, modernist and top-down approach that depicts a liberal 'commercial bourgeoisie' or 'urban oligarchy' dominating governmental and social institutions as instruments to satisfy and perpetuate the status quo and enhance their commercial interests. Perhaps revolutionary at their time, nowadays these studies have become one of the mainstreams of academic historiography on Panamanian national politics and elites. Nevertheless, they have not been able to separate Isthmians' expectations from the sole materialist and economicist aim of taking advantage of Panama's geographical location. The diversity of goals that come from distinct personal experiences, the process of their collectivisation, and their relation to culture or social condition are ignored.

These approaches are teleological because they seek to find sequential manifestations in the past that unravel a story that sustains that Panamanian liberals succeeded in imposing its vision of governance and modernity upon the Isthmian population.[34] The actions of the Panamanian liberal 'bourgeois' are described as a driving force that acquired enough power to materialise their aspiration of exploiting transit through the Isthmus mainly after guiding Panamanians towards independence in 1903. Depending on the writer, the bourgeoisie's expectations are completely fulfilled or not, but they imply that fate of liberalism and liberals was predetermined: they were meant to lead the formation of Panamanian nationhood. Finally, most narratives about the development of Panamanian

---

[31] Ricaurte Soler. *Formas Ideológicas de la Nación Panameña* (Panamá: Ediciones de la Revista "Tareas", 1963) and *Panamá: Oligarquía y Nación, 1925–1972.* (Panamá: Ediciones de la *Revista Tareas,* 1976).

[32] Alfredo Castillero Calvo, 'El movimiento anseatista de 1826. La primera tentativa autonomista de istmeños después de la anexión a Colombia', *Tareas,* No. 4 (Panamá: Imprenta Panamá mayo–jul. 1961).

[33] Alfredo Figueroa Navarro. *Dominio y Sociedad en el Panamá Colombiano (1821–1903)* (Panamá: Impresora Panamá, S.A., 1978).

[34] Thomas Fischer. 'La separación panameña de Colombia a la luz de la historiografía', in *Colombia y Panamá. Metamorfosis de una nación en el siglo XX.* Heraclio Bonilla and Gustavo Montañez, eds. (Bogotá: Universidad Nacional de Colombia, 2004), pp. 333–352.

national identity are also exceptionalist and essentialist. They affirm that Isthmus's geographical position generated a set of experiences which led to the development of an obsession with the enhancement of the inter-oceanic route for commercial purposes. Through time, this mentality became an essential element of Panamanian collective identity and even a kind of unique Isthmian doctrine that Castillero Calvo (and successive authors have) called 'transitism'[35] or, in some cases, 'hanseatism'.[36]

Teleologies of the Panama Canal

There exists a related historiography published in the United States that, directly or indirectly, helped to consolidate the essentialist and exceptionalist narratives of 'transitism' and national liberalism.[37] These studies rarely detach from topics related to the history of the Canal, American triumphalism and the international relations between the United States and Panama. Whether exalting or criticising the impact of the United States' foreign policy and presence in the Isthmus, they build up a historical construction in which American, French, Colombian and Panamanian characters' discourses, imaginaries and deeds are mainly products of the experiences and expectations related to the development of the commercial and military potential of the 'transit zone'. Some of the most significant and widely disseminated examples of this historiography are the books by William D. McCain,[38]

---

[35] Alfredo Castillero Calvo, 'El movimiento anseatista de 1826 ...', p. 10.

[36] The historical source for this article is a document from 1826, in which a group of prominent political and commercial leaders from Panama and other parts of the Republic of Colombia conveyed to the central government their wishes to make Panama a 'Hanseatic country'; referencing the famous medieval confederation of cities in the Baltic. Ibid., p. 4.

[37] See: Rodrigo Miró. 'Hacia una interpretación panameña de nuestra historia', in *Teoría de la Patria.*, En los quinientos años de la Nación Panameña en el Centenario de la República de Panamá. (Panamá: Sociedad Amigos de Panamá, 2003), pp. 2–3.

[38] William D. McCain. *The United States and the Republic of Panama* (Durham, North Carolina: Duke University Press, 1937). In this book, I will use a Spanish version: William D. McCain, *Los Estados Unidos y la República de Panamá*, Nina Shirer, trans. (Panamá: Editorial Universitaria, 1977). Besides accessibility, the Spanish version has a very good preliminary study.

Miles DuVal,[39] Gerstle Mack[40] and David McCollough.[41] They focus on US–Colombian or US–Panamanian relations in the nineteenth and twentieth centuries, and on the quest to build and manage the Panama Canal. Chiefly, they are all *longue durée* approaches that use almost exclusively official and diplomatic sources from the United States concerning the political manoeuvrings linked to the different stages of negotiation about the construction and control of the Canal and the Panama Canal Zone.[42] In contrast to their peers from the United States and Europe, Isthmian (and, in some cases, Colombian) politicians, diplomats, and general population appear either as incompetent or as passive and naïve bystanders.[43] When their interests are taken into account, Panamanian nationalism emerged merely as the result of disappointment with Colombian misgovernance, which, accordingly, neglected the materialisation of a modern future; especially that imagined future linked to having a Canal constructed on Isthmian territory. The teleology arises from the assumption that the unravelling of historical events signalled that the United States would inevitably triumph over nature, construct of the Canal, and consolidate their international supremacy at the beginning of the twentieth century.

These writings have had an important legacy and influenced some Panamanian and other Latin American scholars who take the view that Panamanian identities and nationalisms did not exist before 1903. Good examples of this are the works of lawyer Ovidio Díaz Espino, *El País*

[39] Miles DuVal Jr.. *From Cadiz to Cathay. The Story of the Long Diplomatic Struggle for the Panama Canal.* (Palo Alto: Stanford University Press, 1940). Due to availability, the edition used in this book is the one published by Greenwood Press of New York in 1968.

[40] Gerstle Mack. *The Land Divided. A History of the Panama Canal and Other Isthmian Canal Projects* (New York: Alfred A. Knopff, 1944).

[41] David McCullough. *The Path Between the Seas. The Creation of the Panama Canal. 1870–1914* (New York: Simon and Schuster, 1997).

[42] Out of the 187 documents cited in the bibliography only thirteen were written by Panamanians. Seven of these sources were published after 1930. DuVal, pp. 515–531; In Mack's book, out of 1039 primary and secondary sources, eleven are Panamanian; and in McCollough's book out of 421 sources, five are Panamanian sources. These include two newspapers published in the Isthmus for an English-speaking audience. Among the 198 primary sources consulted, only one was produced by a Panamanian: José Agustín Arango. The rest of the Panamanian sources are an interview and a book on the history of the City of Colón.

[43] Michael L. Conniff. *Panama and the United States. The Forced Alliance* (Athens, Georgia; London: The University of Georgia Press, 1992), p. 65.

creado por Wall Street. La historia prohibida de Panamá y su canal,[44] a summary and paraphrasis of McCollough's book; and of sociologist Olmedo
Beluche, *La verdadera historia de la separación de 1903: reflexiones en torno
al Centenario*[45] and 'La separación de Panamá de Colombia. Mitos y
Falsedades. Reflexiones sobre la Patria'.[46] Beluche correctly indicates that
many of the allegedly nationalist manifestations that occurred in Panama
were actually contemporary to events and consonant with debates occurring in the rest of Colombia. However, this fact does not denies that those
manifestations could carry sincere will to secure local interests. Defining
all members of the Panamanian elites as collaborative with imperialism,
Beluche places the true rise of Panamanian nationalism in popular protests
of the 1920s and nationalist vindications of 1960s. He overlooks that, by
the last quarter of the nineteenth century, expressions of Panamanian
regionalism, proto-nationalism and nationalism became common and
defiant. As for the other Latin American works that follow the similar line,
there is Luis Martínez Delgado's *Panamá: su independencia de España, su
incorporación a la Gran Colombia, su separación de Colombia: el canal
interoceánico*,[47] and Eduardo Lemaitre's relatively well-known *Panamá y
su separación de Colombia*.[48] Both authors are from Colombia. Even
though their story follow the line of Mack and McCollough, they do
grant more relevance to Colombian and Panamanian agency. Their analysis is also nostalgic, for they suggest that both Panama and Colombia
could still be united or have closer relations if their respective leaders had
been less eager to have the Canal built or handled Panamanian affairs and
diplomacy better. In the end, though, both studies do let the reader know
that the construction of the Canal by the United States was unavoidable.

[44] Ovidio Díaz Espino. *El País creado por Wall Street. La historia prohibida de Panamá y su
canal.* Trans. Angela García. (Barcelona: Ediciones Destino, S.A., 2004).
[45] Olmedo Beluche. *La verdadera historia de la separación de 1903: reflexiones en torno al
centenario* (Panamá: Articsa, 2004).
[46] Olmedo Beluche. 'La separación de Panamá de Colombia. Mitos y Falsedades.
Reflexiones sobre la Patria', in *Tareas* No. 122. (Panamá: Centro de Estudios Latinoamericanos
"Justo Arosemena", Enero–Abril, 2006).
[47] Luis Martínez Delgado. *Panamá: su independencia de España, su incorporación a la
Gran Colombia, su separación de Colombia: el canal interoceánico.* (Bogotá: Ediciones
Lerner, 1972).
[48] Eduardo Lemaitre. *Panamá y su separación de Colombia.* (Bogotá: Biblioteca Banco
Popular – Editorial Kelly, 1971).

Panama in the Historiography about Colombia

Most works consulted on Colombian history mention Panama anecdotally.[49] Nonetheless, there are some exceptions that deal with the history of Panama as a region of Colombia in the late nineteenth century.[50] One is William Park's book, *Rafael Núñez and the Politics of Colombian Regionalism, 1863–1886*, which analyses Rafael Núñez's life in Panama and his connections to Panamanian elites.[51] Another relevant example is Helen Delpar's *Red Against Blue. The Liberal Party in Colombian Politics, 1863–1899*. Her book draws heavily upon source material from Buenaventura Correoso's personal papers.[52] In 2004, the Universidad Nacional de Colombia published the proceedings of a conference called, *Panamá y Colombia: Metamorfosis de una Nación*.[53] This is an important contribution to the existing historiography, because it incorporates new analysis from the perspectives of social and cultural history and represents an effort to connect the history of both countries.

Historiography on Panamanian and Colombian Conservatism

The sources that discuss the role of Conservatives in Panama generally describe them as an oligarchic group of large rural landowners and descendants of Spanish colonial bureaucrats. Soler and Figueroa Navarro indicate that conservatives were opposed to the liberal 'urban oligarchy' or 'commercial bourgeoisie' and the inhabitants of the *arrabal*.[54] For Figueroa Navarro, their economic practices in rural areas engendered relationships

[49] See: Bushnell, *The Making of Modern Colombia.*; Marco Palacios. *Between Legitimacy and Violence. A History of Colombia, 1875–2002.* (Durham and London: Duke University Press, 2006); and Marco Palacios and Frank Safford. *Colombia: Fragmented Land, Divided Society* (New York: Oxford University Press, 2001).

[50] For the early nineteenth century see: Marixa Lasso. *Myths of Harmony: Race and Republicanism during the Age of Revolution, Colombia, 1795–1831.* (Pittsburgh: University of Pittsburgh Press, 2007).

[51] James W. Park. *Rafael Núñez and the Politics of Colombian Regionalism, 1863–1886.* (Baton Rouge and London: Louisiana State University Press, 1985).

[52] Helen Delpar. *Red Against Blue. The Liberal Party in Colombian Politics, 1863–1899.* (Alabama: The University of Alabama Press, 1981).

[53] *Colombia y Panamá. Metamorfosis de una nación en el siglo XX.* Heraclio Bonilla and Gustavo Montañez, ed. (Bogotá: Universidad Nacional de Colombia, 2004).

[54] Ibid. Also see: Soler, *Pensamiento.* p. 43. Aparicio. 'Represión y explotación', pp. 240–241.

of feudal lordship.[55] Contradictorily, he recognises that Panamanian conservatives and liberals interacted commercially and socially,[56] as many the former in Panama had professional degrees and careers.[57] Historian Fernando Aparicio argues that certain economic policies implemented during *La Regeneración* were restrictive and negative for the Panamanian 'service economy'.[58] Intellectually, conservatives are presented as a reactionary minority with a blind attachment to religion and without much interest in models of scientific, social and economic modernisation.[59] Soler argues there was only a small group of conservative and 'anti-positivist' thinkers in Panama, who promoted a 'new vogue … of colonial thinking' that had 'retrogressive tendencies'.[60] Although he attributes this reactionary group insignificant innovations, Soler reluctantly admits that they were capable of reconfiguring 'old dogmas'.[61]

There are enough studies that nuance the image of conservatives as a mainly rural group that countered modernisation and possessed retrograde beliefs. Already in 1987, Christopher Abel demonstrated that there were 'conciliatory groups' and 'pacifist factions' amongst the political parties of Colombia.[62] Abel claims that by the 1880s these factions allied and controlled political power. Their project, *La Regeneración*, was, at least

---

[55] Figueroa Navarro, *Dominio y Sociedad*, pp. 101–102.

[56] Ibid., pp. 123–125.

[57] Alfredo Figueroa Navarro. 'El departamento de colombiano de Panamá a fines del siglo diecinueve e inicios de la vigésima centuria'. *Colombia y Panamá. Metamorfosis de una nación en el siglo XX*. Heraclio Bonilla and Gustavo Montañez, ed. (Bogotá: Universidad Nacional de Colombia, 2004), p. 105. For a similar observation see: Armando Múñoz Pinzón *'El Conflicto Azuereño de 1854'* in *Historia General de Panamá*. Vol. II. Tomo III. Capítulo V. Castillero Calvo, Alfredo (ed.) (Panamá: Comité del Centenario de la República, 2004), p. 176.

[58] Aparicio, p. 245.

[59] Figueroa, *Dominio y Sociedad.*, p. 232.

[60] Ricaurte Soler. *Pensamiento Panameño y Concepción de la Nacionalidad durante el siglo XIX* (para la historia de las ideas en el Istmo). 2da. Edición. (Panamá: Librería Cultural Panameña, S.A., 1971), pp. 42–43. For Soler's views on twentieth-century conservatism see: Ricaurte Soler. *Panamá: Nación y Oligarquía 1925–1975.* (Panamá: Ediciones de la Revista Tareas, 1976), pp. 15 and 42.

[61] Ibid., p. 43. For similar interpretations see: César Julio González Herrera. *Aproximación Historiográfica al Pensamiento Ideológico-Político del Conservadurismo en Panamá*, (Panamá: Editorial Mariano Arosemena – Instituto Nacional de Cultura, 2003). This book won the essay section of the Ricardo Miró, Panama's National Contest of Literature.

[62] Christopher Abel. *Política, Iglesia y Partidos en Colombia 1886–1953* (Bogotá: FAES – Universidad de Colombia, 1987), p. 17.

rhetorically, presented as a reform seeking the 'elimination of sectarian passions' and 'the end of political provocation'.[63]

Beyond Colombia, Charles A. Hale's analysis of *La Reforma* and the transformation of liberalism in Mexico illustrates how many liberals were inspired by the ideas of Saint Simon and Auguste Comte's positivism,[64] and the Conservative governments of France and Spain under Adolphe Thiers, Jules Simon and Emilio Castelar.[65] Hale states that, drawing from these ideas, they created a positivist liberalism which advocated the application of 'scientific politics',[66] which, supposedly, pinpointed the problems of the country and formulated its political action in a scientific way. The main aims of their policies were: to attack doctrinary liberalism or 'metaphysical politics'; to promote of a strong government that could withstand revolutions and anarchy; and to make a call for constitutional reform. In addition, Hale argues that another of their objectives was to conciliate political divisions; and that conservatives were the first to offer some sort of conciliation across the board.[67] Hence, this transformed liberalism which took into consideration many conservative principles,[68] and could thus be defined as a sort of 'conservatised liberalism'.[69] This alignment was possible because not all conservatives were against positivism or cooperation with liberals.

On another aspect of the political panorama, Eduardo Posada-Carbó questions the narratives that present the centralisation of the state during *La Regeneración* as an instrument capable of monitoring and manipulating the electoral system with absolute effectiveness. He points out that this method of control was not unchallengeable, because there was no well-organised electoral machinery or party cohesion. Besides, there were many dissidents.[70] The president and his ministers could certainly name the departmental governors, but their authority 'particularly in distant prov-

[63] Ibid., p. 18.
[64] Charles A. Hale. *La transformación del liberalismo en México a fines del siglo XIX.* (México: Fondo de Cultura Económica, 2002), pp. 24 and 53. For a classic on Latin American positivism read: Leopoldo Zea. *El positivismo en México: Nacimiento, apogeo y decacencia.* (México: Fondo de Cultura Económica, 1968).
[65] Hale, pp. 53 and 72–73.
[66] Ibid., p. 50.
[67] Ibid., pp. 24–25.
[68] Ibid., pp. 67–68.
[69] Ibid., pp. 66–67 and 117.
[70] Posada-Carbó, p. 262 and 265.

inces' could be defied by locally elected authorities and the even the selected governors themselves.[71] The Conservative hegemony also had to confront electoral fraud.[72] Finally, Posada-Carbó claims that the restrictions placed on voting for electores and representatives (knowing how to read and write, or having an annual income of 500,00 pesos, or owning property worth 1,500 pesos) by **Article 173** had 'lost their original meaning' because many people of middle-income 'managed to fulfill the requirement'.[73] Furthermore, 'male universal suffrage was accepted for local elections'.[74] In sum, the Conservative leaders of *La Regeneración* were not able to completely monopolise the political system or govern without any opposition.[75]

Some authors have shown that the conservatives were not opposed to science and technology. Frank Safford sustains that they may have been fervourous supporters of the Church and opposed to liberal ideas, but they did not entirely discard scientific and practical education and knowledge.[76] Similarly, in *Modernization in Colombia: The Laureano Gómez Years, 1889–1965,* James Henderson argues that during and after *La Regeneración* there were several conservative individuals who tried to promote technology and science in order to advance their idea of progress in Colombia.[77]

Eugene Davis discusses how conservative policies combined positivism with Catholic social thought, especially Jaime Balmes' philosophy. Although Latin American thought is often perceived as 'revolutionary', he states that the region has 'also felt the impact of a different stream of creative thought in Hispanic and Christian traditionalism',[78] which responded to 'the invasion of utilitarian, Utopian, Liberal and … positivist and

---

[71] Ibid., p. 265
[72] Ibid., p. 267.
[73] Ibid, pp. 258–259.
[74] Ibid., p. 258.
[75] To see a study of conservatives as a democratic force see in Chile: Samuel J. Valenzuela, 'Class Relations and Democratization. A reassessment of Barrington Moore's Model', Miguel Ángel Centeno and Fernando López-Alves, ed. *The Other Mirror. Grand Theory Through the Lens of Latin America.* (Princeton and Oxford: Princeton University Press, 2001).
[76] Frank Safford. *The Ideal of the Practical,* pp. 16–17.
[77] James Henderson. *Modernization in Colombia: The Laureano Gómez Years, 1889–1965.* (Gainesville: University of Florida Press, 2001), pp. 16–18.
[78] Harold Eugene Davis. 'Jaime Balmes, Spanish Traditionalist: His Influence in Spanish America', *The Americas,* Vol. 35, No. 3 Academy of American Franciscan History: January 1979), p. 341. http://www.jstor.org/stable/980978

Marxist theories'. For Colombia, Davis shows that Miguel Antonio Caro and his father José Eusebio Caro (founder of the Conservative Party in Colombia) belonged to this group of conservative intellectuals. Ultimately, Davis affirms not all of them were radical reactionaries and that they have not 'always defended absolute monarchy, a hierarchical structure of society and the special prerogatives of the Church and the Army'. More importantly, he asserts that studying how Conservatives in Spanish America accepted Catholic social thought can help to understand the evolution of liberalism in Spanish America, for many of its advocates became positivists and later allied with moderate conservatives, as was the relevant case of Rafael Núñez.[79]

Following the bibliography above, I will argue that conservatives in nineteenth-century Colombia and Panama were more dynamic than is commonly assumed and participated actively in the political, social, economic and cultural spheres. As a result, their actions certainly had an impact in Panamanian nation-formation, state-building and cultural trends, especially taking into account that they dominated politics in Colombian Panama from at least 1886.

Review of History of Education

This monograph highlights the shortage of books, chapters and articles about the history of Panamanian education. Most of them emphasise the supposed hegemony of liberal ideas in Panamanian pedagogical thought, the poor condition of schools in 'Colombian Panama', and the legal evolution of education policies.[80] These secondary sources share very limited

[79] Ibid. p. 343. Also see: Jesús Ferro Bayón. 'Núñez y la filosofía política. Apuntes para una historia de las ideas en la Costa', Gustavo Bell Lemus, comp. *El Caribe Colombiano. Selección de textos históricos.* (Barranquilla: Ediciones Uninorte, 1988), pp. 223–227.
[80] Some of the most important are Alfredo Cantón. *Desenvolvimiento de las Ideas Pedagógicas en Panamá. 1903–1926.* (Panamá: Imprenta Nacional, 1955); Andrés Culiolis. *500 años de Educación en Panamá. Análisis crítico-político.* (Madrid and Panamá: Editora Escolar, S.A. – Susaeta Ediciones, S.A., 1992); Francisco S. Céspedes Alemán. *La Educación en Panamá: panorama histórico y antología.* (Panamá: Imprenta Universitaria Biblioteca Cultural Panameña, 1981). Juan Bosco Bernal. 'La Educación en Panamá: antecedentes, tendencias y perspectivas', *Panamá: Cien Años de República.* (Panamá: Manfer, S.A., 2004). José Alberto Del Cid Felipe. *Desarrollo de la Educación General y los inicios de la Universidad de Panamá.* (Panamá: Imprenta de la Universidad de Panamá, 2013).

information about history of education in Panama during the nineteenth century. They do indicate that Panamanian educators of the period were influenced by the ideas of Swiss pedagogue Johann Hienrich Pestalozzi[81] and German educator Johann Friedrich Herbart.[82] In addition, they do provide information related to early attempts to establish a proper education system in Panama, the name of influential individuals, and numbers of schools and students in the Isthmus. However, many of these sources are not immune to nationalist biases or to the teleologies of liberalism. On the one hand, guided by pedagogue Octavio Méndez Pereira's publication, *El Desarrollo de la Instrucción Pública en Panamá* (*The Development of Public Instruction in Panama*) of 1916, the subsequent studies claim, without making an extensive analysis, that nineteenth-century Panamanian education was very poor due to defective governance from Bogotá. On the other hand, based on the assumption that liberal ideas dominated intellectual life in Panama, most of these secondary sources seldom observe the changes in education policy that occurred during the period *La Regeneración* and rarely analyse to what extent its premises were absorbed by teachers, students and the population in general. They do not explore the importance of ideas and how they shaped the content of the curricula or courses or affected teaching-learning dynamics in schools and classrooms. This book represents a first attempt to reach those details that can enrich our comprehension of history of Panamanian social and intellectual life in the late nineteenth and early twentieth centuries.

CONCEPTS, THEORIES AND METHODOLOGY

In order to contribute to previous and current debates and to sustain my arguments, I resorted to several works on the history of nationalism, education, knowledge, Latin American intellectuals, conceptual history, and sociology.

The Cosmopolitan Reason and Progress

Thomas Popkewitz's explorations of the 'cosmopolitan reason' are key to understanding the conductive ideology and projects of the Isthmian pedagogical elite. According to him, cosmopolitanism arose during the

---

[81] Céspedes, p. 37; Culiolis, p. 73.
[82] Bernal, p. 56.

Enlightenment. It proposes that humankind could come together in complete unity through the work of agents that act in accordance with science
and reason.[83] Nevertheless, Popkewitz argues, the cosmopolitan reason
has 'double-gestures'.[84] On one side, 'cosmopolitanism' includes people
with similar behaviours, knowledges, skills and values deemed as related to
'reasonability'.[85] On the other side, it produces 'projects of abjection' by
defining those who do not exactly fit into the cosmopolitan formula as
'unreasonable' or inferior.[86] In this sense, it is common to see cosmopolitan values appropriated when a collective claims reasonability, common
sense and scientific thought as part of its idiosyncrasy.[87] According to
Popkewitz, this becomes a story of exceptionalism. Those who appropri-
ate cosmopolitanism in the name of a particular collective do so because
they perceive that alterity is an impediment to their progress.[88] In other
words, this paves the way towards the double gestures of cosmopolitanism: there is the inclusion of those who, allegedly, are capable to contribute to the construction of a homogenised world; and, there is seclusion of
those who, supposedly, impede humanity to united under one standardised
view of civilisation. Education has the goal of neutralising these external
menaces by transforming or normalising otherness through partial adaptation, absorption or adoption. In Colombian Panama, the policies to eradicate or exacerbate the conflicts related to politics, religion, ethnicity, or the
social behaviour of the majorities are an example of these 'projects of
abjection'.

Connecting this to Reinhart Kosselleck's writings, I argue that the original and most pristine sense of 'horizon of expectations' of 'cosmopolitan
reason' entailed the unification of all humanity. The deferral of such a
universal amalgamation generate perceptions of failure. This is the result
of 'spaces of experience' that are interpreted as moments of crisis, decline,
de-acceleration in the search for progress or modernity.[89] Kosselleck's and
Popkewitz's theories further expound that times conceived as periods of

[83] Thomas S. Popkewitz. *Cosmopolitanism and the Age of School Reform. Science, Education, and the Making of the Child.* (New York: Routledge, 2008), p. 16.

[84] Ibid., p. 12.

[85] Ibid., pp. 4 and 28.

[86] Ibid., pp. 28 and 35.

[87] Ibid., pp. 3 and 46.

[88] Ibid., pp. 12 and 15.

[89] Reinhart Kosselleck. *Futures Past. On the Semantics of Historical Time.* Keith Tribe, trans. (New York: Columbia University Press, 2004), p. 269.

crisis, regression or stagnation might evoke pessimism or fear of danger. This was the discourse of Núñez when he manifested a sense of peril by calling for regeneration as a way to prevent catastrophe. Sometimes, these notions of decadence generate the idea that chaos is necessary to progress even faster. Similarly, stories of success never completely materialise positive visions of the future. In response, new horizons of expectations are established.[90] This transformation involves a reconfiguration of concepts such as 'progress' and 'regress'.[91] With the changes of discursive conditions provoked by new positive or negative experiences, failure and partial success can be reconstituted to be a sign of hope centred around the notion that, provided there is sufficient rationality and hard work, after making the required adjustments, human agents can enact a level of 'perfectibility' in line with collective expectations for the realisation of the ideal of progress.[92]

In this manuscript I will argue that this is a demonstration that there is no fear of progress itself, but of following a mistaken route that lead to an illusion of progress and, thus, chaos. In connection to this, this study will present evidence how perceived 'decline' and subsequent adjustments do not necessarily create a will to reach a better unknown moment in the future, but often engenders a wish to return to a supposed better moment in the past from which humankind should restart its journey towards an ideal world.

Education and Modernity in Panama

Understanding the way intellectuals conceptualised modernity and progress is essential to study their social and cultural priorities. In her *Re-Inventing Modernity in Latin America. Intellectuals Imagine the Future (1900–1930)*, Nicola Miller analyses how Latin American intellectuals relay state-making into their visions of modernity. In order to explain her points, she differentiates between the terms 'modernisation' and 'modernity'. The

---

[90] Reinhart Kosselleck, *The Practice of Conceptual History. Timing History, Spacing Concepts.* Todd Samuel Presner et al., trans. (Stanford: Stanford University Press, 2002), p. 233; Popkewitz, p. 34.

[91] Koselleck, *The Practice* ..., pp. 218–219. For the importance of language in the construction of these concepts see: Miguel Ángel Cabrera. *Historia, Lenguaje y Teoría de la Sociedad,* (Valencia: Frónesis Cátedra Universitat de Valencia, 2001), p. 116.

[92] Kosselleck. *The Practice* ..., pp. 227–228.

former represents 'processes, which are objectively measurable by positivist methods', such as

> capital formation and the emergence of capitalist relations of production; industrialization and urbanization; the privileging of empirical science and its associated technology as the prime source of knowledge; state bureaucratization; secularization; commitment to impersonality of the law; the promotion of individualism; the separation of public and private spheres; and the advent of mass politics.[93]

Following Miller's arguments, education is, indeed, about measuring the number of new schools, teachers and students, new professionals, or calculating the amount of 'useful' knowledge taught and learnt (for example, literacy) in hours and credits and summative evaluations. Furthermore, and more importantly, without education, planning, calculating and measuring modernisation would be improbable.

Miller also presented a dual definition of 'modernity'. She writes that

> in its inbuilt relativity, modernity represents a state that is always achievable, but always deferred ... In its inherent subjectivity, [it] is about ways of perceiving, understanding, and imagining the world ... Modernity's generic promise is that historical transformation can be brought about by rational human agency, conquering space and time (i.e., geography and history) through scientific knowledge to create a society of greater justice, sovereignty, and liberty.[94]

According to Miller, in the nineteenth century, Latin American intellectuals developed a notion that she calls 'technocratic modernity' which promotes 'an ideology of progress defined primarily in economic terms, driven by instrumental reason and technology, and implemented by a knowledge elite'. However, she also describes a transition in Latin Americans' definition of modernity by the end of the nineteenth century. She utilises the term 'alternative modernity' to describe a view on modernity 'committed to reason and progress but seeking to realize [its]

---

[93] Nicola Miller. *Re-inventing Modernity in Latin America, 1900–1930.* (New York: Palgrave Macmillan, 2008), p. 4.
[94] Ibid.

emancipatory potential."[95] This was the result of a Latin American realisation that they had to produce hybrid models to materialise modernity. Intrinsically, 'modernisation' is loaded with values that define how each person or collective delimit the right kind of progress and modernity. Because of this, modernising and progressing go beyond a mere seeking for technological development or commercial advantage. They involve looking for a consolidation of acceptable social behaviours and lifestyles within a so-called civilised frame of morality. Whether they aimed for 'technocratic' or 'alternative' modernity, Latin American intellectuals imagined that conducting a correct process of modernisation will guarantee reaching the highest level of civilisation. In this fashion, they could demonstrate that their collectives (the political party, city, province, country, nation, etc.) had interiorised the cosmopolitan reason, a requisite to get transnational and international recognition and negotiate in equal terms with the leaders of the world.

However, the constant adjustments that education undergoes, such as the one seeing during *La Regeneración*, implies that there is a persistent perception that modernity has been deferred. It signifies a fear not of modernity, but of undertaking the wrong form of modernisation. This is shown in the transition from 'technocratic' to 'alternative' modernity in Latin America, which proposed slightly different methods of schooling. That is, the many educational reforms illustrate that there is always hope and confidence that through the agents of education (teachers and students) a better society could be consolidated.

Cultural Capital, Social Space and Habitus

Pierre Bourdieu's discussion about education and cultural capital links arguments about the appropriations of the cosmopolitan reason (and their related 'projects of adbjection' and 'double gestures'), the possession of certain knowledges, and the rise of the pedagogical elite in Panama.[96] Bourdieu claims that the possession of certain forms of cultural capital

---

[95] Ibid., pp. 10–11.

[96] Pierre Bourdieu. 'What Makes a Social Class? On the Theoretical and Practical Existence of Groups' in *Berkeley Journal of Sociology*, Vol. 32 (Berkeley: Regents of the University of California: 1987), pp. 1–2 and 4. Also see, Pierre Bourdieu. 'Espacio Social y Espacio Simbólico. Introducción a una lectura japonesa de *la distinción*' in *Capital cultural, escuela y espacio social*. Isabel Jiménez, trans. (Avellaneda, Argentina: Siglo Veintiuno Editores, S.A., 2008), p. 35.

defines the position of a person in society.[97] Individuals who have similar cultural capital are close to each other on Bourdieu's famous graph of social spaces. These actors probably have similar *habitus*.[98] Inside the education system, educators who establish themselves as leaders of the pedagogical elite institutionalise 'double gestures': they might include or change the social space, the cultural capital and even the *habitus* of their disciples, but can also reproduce the hegemony of certain kinds of knowledge.[99] This preservation of status and cultural capital is synonymous with the awarding and obtaining of degrees, which constitutes a certification of knowledgeability and of belonging to intellectual spheres;[100] a diploma is the key to entering or remaining in dominant intellectual social spaces. Despite basing their work on science and reason and sharing similar social spaces, leading sectors society (including educators themselves) attribute more scientific value to their own knowledge and ideas. This implies rejecting those who do not share the same knowledges, ideas and interests.

Similarly, the curricula, course content and schools are not always designed to provide equal cultural capital. The whole illusion of homogenising a collective through education is built upon the notion of inclusion that brings all the members of the group together for their benefit. Public education promises to democratise learning: students will acquire the same cultural capital as their fellow classmates after finishing the programme, so social space and *habitus* differences will cease to exist. Nevertheless, the fact that different kinds of schools private and public; lay and religious; primary and secondary; teachers' schools; commerce schools; arts and crafts schools; all-girls and all-men schools; military academies; and universities that are founded already break with this ideal, as all these types of institutions would follow distinct teaching methods, programmes and courses; they would have different invented traditions. It is likely that those who follow the school's rules and methods would rise within the public education system, either as student or as teacher.

Bourdieu's notion of 'social spaces' allows for individuals from distinct social situations establishing collaborative networks.[101] For him, a person might acquire new knowledges and behaviours, and thus move to

---

[97] Bourdieu. 'What Makes a Social Class? …', pp. 4–5.
[98] Ibid., p. 5.
[99] Bourdieu. 'Nuevo capital … pp, 95–98
[100] Ibid., p. 98.
[101] Bourdieu, 'Espacio Social y Espacio Simbólico …', p. 29.

different social spaces and transform their *habitus*, can develop similar interests, emotions, thoughts and beliefs. At the same time, it is possible to argue that people in similar social spaces and with common *habitus* can disaggregate. But, all these changes do not come into being from nothing. As Kosselleck states, 'spaces of experience' and the thoughts and beliefs engendered from them have to be taken into account to understand how individuals and collectives perceive their current situation and envision the future. This might motivate mobility within social spaces, a will to acquire new cultural capital and a change individual social conditions. In this sense, education is key. If its purpose is to progress and realise modernity or prevent crisis and recover from it, then its main goal is not necessarily to reproduce knowledge and the social status quo. This would mean stagnation or decline. Instead, the main objective of schools is to change the students' cultural capital and *habitus* with the promise that their future would also evolve in a positive way. Improvements in a person's condition does not mean reaching equality, though. Each kind of teaching institution and teacher would follow distinct programmes and courses, implement various teaching-learning methods, promote the practice of particular invented traditions. It is likely that those who adapt and navigate the best within the education system would rise.

The Worth of Knowledge

This book also elaborates on the works of Peter Burke concerning the history of knowledge.[102] Following them, I assert that there is no historical unrestrained production and accumulation of knowledge.[103] Instead, the approval or marginalisation of certain knowledges determines which of them are produced or accumulated;[104] which are to be discarded and forgotten;[105] and sometimes, which ought to be rescued or recovered.[106] This book posits that this requires a process of choosing and training of teachers or of those who transmit knowledge, along with the selection of the students and children who are worthy of acquiring it.

[102] Peter Burke. *What is History of Knowledge?* (Cambridge: Polity Press, 2016).
[103] Burke, pp. 15–17.
[104] Ibid. p. 29–37.
[105] Ibid., p. 52–55
[106] Ibid., pp. 42, 47, 61–63, and 104.

All these developments are associated with ideological, political and intellectual trends which create temporal surges and demarcations into what constitutes a 'valuable' type of knowledge; be that moral, religious, technical, scientific or humanist. Within this frame, this discrimination of knowledge is allegedly necessary in order to modernise or progress. Thus, educational debates largely revolve around the best method to instil and preserve a form of information and how present it to different audiences.[107] During *La Regeneración*, the role of the Panamanian pedagogical elite was to design instruments to instil a conservative perspective of modernity and progress, a prerogative that compelled educators to emphasise the teaching of Catholic morals and officially approved scientific, technical and practical knowledges.

Intellectuals, Pedagogues and Modernity

Who are the members of this pedagogical elite? Nicola Miller's explanations of the evolution of intellectual life in Latin America between the nineteenth and twentieth centuries are essential to clarify and contextualise the characteristics of these agents of authority in Panama between 1878 and 1903. In the nineteenth century, 'the exclusivity of … education had enabled a minority from the socio-economic elite to combine intellectual and political authority.'[108] She explains that there were distinct forms of intellectual behaviour, but all of Panamanian educators and most intellectuals belonged to the group she calls '*licenciados-políticos*'.[109] They were persons who, generally speaking, possessed secondary school education and had taken some higher education courses and even had graduated from universities. Many of them were certified professionals. They were people who had access to modern knowledge via books, lectures, cultural societies, *tertulias* and libraries. This facilitated their access to positions of power.

But, as Miller explains, there was a transition from 'The generalist *letrado* of the [nineteenth century] … who moved freely between politics and literature, playing multiple roles as ideologue, legislator, educator,

---

[107] Ibid, pp. 77.

[108] Nicola Miller. *In the Shadow of the State. Intellectuals and the Quest for National Identity in Twentieth-century Spanish America.* (London and New York: Verso, 1999), p. 6.

[109] She also mentions the *caudillo-pensador*, who was a leader, usually military—and a thinker. Miller, *In the Shadow of the State*, p. 6.

scholar' to 'a modern, specialist *letrado*'.[110] Indeed, in late nineteenth-century Panama, the intellectual sphere witnessed a period of transformation when the *licenciado-político*, who were initially involved in governing education, began to give way to a class of professional pedagogues who had graduated from *escuelas normales* and universities. According to Miller, this happened because 'modernization began to introduce a degree of professionalization into intellectual activity, opening up opportunities for people from outside the elites to earn a living ... from intellectual work'.[111] Some of the main agents studied in this book were not members of the classical political, economic or social elites, but managed to become leading intellectuals and educators. Their position as intellectuals gradually permitted some of them to obtain political, social and economic capital and enter elitist spheres.

Although some of these actors advocated for the autonomy of pedagogues and received profit from other professional activities (journalism, lawyers, engineering, medicine, etc.), all them worked at one time or another, if not during all their lives, for the state. They probably did this consciously and willingly, because, as Miller claims, the 'fate of Spanish American intellectuals remained bound up with the interventionist state, even when they defined themselves in opposition to it – not only because they were often dependent upon it for employment, but also because it offered the only route to the realization of their visions'.[112] In order to be able to place themselves under the 'shadow of the state', Isthmian pedagogues had to share or pretend to share the same postures and visions of those who controlled the government. They also had to transmit a particular kind of cultural capital. In the official language of late nineteenth-century Panama, imparting knowledge was thought to enhance the conservative and moderate liberal alliance's views of modernity. This partially excludes priests and nuns, for, even when they had the required degrees, cultural capital and networks, their allegiance was to the Church rather than to the state. In certain way, at least temporarily, priest and nuns were members of an ecclesiastical pedagogical elite, but, in the case of Panama, many of those who initially thrived left at the eve of the War of the Thousand Days.

---

[110] Nicola Miller. *Re-inventing Modernity* ... p. 7.
[111] Miller, *In the Shadow of the State*, p. 6.
[112] Ibid., p. 6.

In contrast, civilian pedagogues remained in their positions, some advanced professionally, and they kept more permanent impact on Isthmian Public Instructions.

The Image of Children

Based on the works by Miguel Pereyra, Thomas Popkewitz and Barry Franklin,[113] this study analyses how students are viewed by the educational authorities, pedagogues and adults in general. In Popkewitz's writings, the identity of children is construed metaphorically. From one perspective, they are represented as the future of the collective.[114] That is, children represent hope; a sort of raw material who through education can help a group to fulfil its expectations, i.e., recover from crisis, prevent catastrophe or maintain due course on the path of progress towards modernity.[115] From another viewpoint, children are deemed as people who have yet to become reasonable and who require education to become scientifically-minded, well-mannered and productive agents of society. In other words, they are outside of the cosmopolitan realm. In this sense, children could be seen as dangerous.[116] Adults project their fears onto them, perceiving that uneducated or miseducated children will become unreasonable adults and a cause of decadence in the future. Youth needs to be oriented and tamed to become good citizens and problems-solvers.[117] This is the basis for the development of the 'salvation narratives' of schooling: the idea that education leads to the salvation of a society as well as the notion that education needs to be saved through reforms and adjustments led by the pedagogical elite.[118]

---

[113] Barry M. Franklin, Miguel A. Pereyra and Thomas S. Popkewitz. 'History, the Problem of Knowledge, and the New Cultural History of Schooling: An Introduction' in *Cultural History and Education. Critical Essays on Knowledge and Schooling.* Barry M. Franklin, Miguel A. Pereyra, and Thomas S. Popkewitz eds. (New York: Routledgefalmer, 2001), pp. 3–42.; and Antonio Novoa. 'Writing "New" Histories of Education', in *Cultural History and Education. Critical Essays on Knowledge and Schooling.* Barry M. Franklin, Miguel A. Pereyra, and Thomas S. Popkewitz eds. (New York: Routledgefalmer, 2001), pp. 45–66.

[114] Popkewitz, pp. 31–33.

[115] Ibid., p. 33.

[116] Ibid., p. 32.

[117] Ibid., pp. 28 and 33.

[118] Ibid., pp. 28–29; also see, Franklin, Pereyra, and Popkewitz, p. 17.

The Construction of Professional, Partisan and National Identities

In order to understand how politicians, intellectuals and the pedagogical elite worked towards the creation of identities during *La Regeneración*, this monograph draws from the seminal works on nationalism by Anthony Smith, Erich Hobsbawm and Benedict Anderson. The first author's studies on ethnic and civic nationalism, as well as his conception of ethnosymbolic reconstruction as an fundamental element for the survival of national identities helped to see how, during *La Regeneración*, a recodification of Catholic and Hispanic traditionalism adopted the language of positivism to give the reform a sense of national cohesion. This reconfiguration of civil and ethnic national discourse formulated an image that presented *La Regeneración* as a new and true liberation process that would finally concede peacefulness, order and modernisation to Colombia.[119] Benedict Anderson's analysis shows the importance of print-capitalism and schooling as a mean to create a cohesive nation. Regarding this, he writes that 'the newspaper is an "extreme form" of the book ... sold on a colossal scale, but of ephemeral popularity'.[120] This was reinforced through the self-assurance that generates from mimicking their peers' behaviours. That is, members of a professional group, political party, a larger community tend to emulate their partners' patterns of information consumption as it produces a sense of belonging.[121] Albeit the ephemerality of the newspaper implies that the events and personages described in the news might be forgotten, the constant reading of the same editorial line also means that the reader is repetitiously exposed to the same discourse. This means that even if a periodical existed for a short period of time, its writers' message was not always transitory.

The case of Panama and Colombia is similar to what Halperín Donghi identified in the case of Argentina, where political leaders, such as Juan Manuel Rosas, used print-capitalism to 'implant an "imagined community" in the collective consciousness', but instead 'the community was not

---

[119] Anthony Smith. *Nationalism. Theory, Ideology, History.* (Cambridge and Massachusetts: Polity Press, 2008), pp. 39–42, 57, and 84–85.

[120] Benedict Anderson. *Imagined Communites. Reflections on the Origin and Spread of Nationalism.* (London and New York: Verso, 2006), p. 34.

[121] Ibid., pp. 35–36.

to be the *patria* but the party ...'.[122] Partisan newspapers presented their leaders' plans as true national interests, while those of the rival parties were defined as dangerous. In late nineteenth-century Colombian Panama, the collective act of reading factional but regional newspapers had a dual result. Just as Anderson wrote, receiving news about co-partisans and rivals in other parts of the country formed a consciousness of its particular national situations, allowing Colombians and Panamanians to recognise each other as members of the same nation. Paradoxically, the regional and partisan character of many newspapers derived from political discrepancies and regionalism. Hence, the daily mass ceremony of reading politicised newspapers (or any form of printed material) helped to place the members of political factions either in favour or against the national programme and ideals of *La Regeneración*, diluting the strengthening of nation-cohesion.

In respect to the importance of schools in the formation of identities, Anderson indicates that the public education system 'formed a colossal, highly rationalized, tightly centralized hierarchy, structurally analogous to the state bureaucracy itself. Uniform, text-books, standardized diplomas and teaching certificates, a strictly regulated gradation of age-groups, classes and instructional materials, in themselves created a self-contained, coherent universe of experience.'[123] This means that, in spite the governments attempted to regulate education, the schooling system could become a parallel imagined community, where certain individuals or groups may challenge the projects of nation-building from within, while still being part of the official system as organic intellectuals.

Anderson's assertions about the ceremonial reading of the newspapers also applies to school textbooks. The act of reading the same textbooks everyday might be ephemeral in many senses: students could see the content as tedious and uninteresting and their attention could fade away, so the class and the lesson could be easily forgotten. Nonetheless, differently from the newspapers, some textbooks are read by several generations of

---

[122] Tulio Halperín Donghi. 'Argentina Counterpoint: Rise of Nation, Rise of the State', *Beyond Imagined Communities. Reading and Writing the Nation in Nineteenth-Century Latin America*. John Charles Chasteen and Sara Castro-Klarén, eds. (Washington, D.C., Baltimore and London: Woodrow Wilson Center Press – The Johns Hopkins University Press, 2003), p. 46. Also see: Eduardo Posasa-Carbó. 'Newspapers, Politics, and Election in Colombia, 1830–1930' in *The Historical Journal* (Cambridge: Cambridge University Press, December, 2010), Vol. 53., No. 4 , pp. 939–962 Stable URL: https://www.jstor.org/stable/40930364

[123] Anderson, p. 121.

students. They learn and take tests based on those books (and sometimes on their successive new editions). The textbook may resist obsoleteness.

Hobsbawm's work on invented traditions also sheds light on how the repetitive practices occurring within schools, such as singing the national or school anthem, reading and studying of the same books, having classes with the same teacher, and taking the same courses over time becomes a tradition, or more exactly, a routine that guides students to symbolically 'follow in the footsteps' of prestigious professors and previous successful graduates.[124] Graduating symbolises that a student had properly followed the teacher's instructions and learned the content of courses and their textbooks and lectures. It signifies an individual and collective achievement. The whole process towards obtaining a degree contains a set of follow up sub-traditions: taking and passing final exams, attend a graduation ceremony, among others. Even when in many cases it meant making an effort for yielding to the disciplinary regulations of the school and of passing through many (sometimes tedious) hours of classes and studying, these are events imagined as a rituals of passage. It represents the beginning of more prosperous times or of an illustrious career. In the line of Franklin, Pereyra and Popkewitz, it is also a metaphor that means that the children have become fully civilised through the agency and taming of the education system.

METHODOLOGY AND SOURCES

To corroborate the feasibility of these conceptual and theoretical frameworks, I applied qualitative and quantitative methodologies to analyse a relatively wide collection of primary sources: political pamphlets, newspapers and periodicals, compilations of essays, official reports, public speeches, poetry, information about the teachers' ideas, the curricula, and methods of assessment. One of the major challenges to writing this book was the lack of detailed information about the events occurring in the classrooms and the scarce number of reliable biographies. Most of the existing life stories have been sponsored and tend to praise an individual. There are some 'official' compilations of short biographies, but they generally have very fragmentary information and the same purpose. Even

---

[124] Eric Hobsbawm. 'Inventing Traditions' in *The Invention of Tradition*, Eric Hobsbawm and Terence Ranger, eds. 20th printing (Cambridge: Cambridge University Press, 2012), pp. 2 and 9.

worse, since the 1920s, Panamanian historiography began to concentrate only on the lives of a few characters, especially those considered national heroes (or anti-heroes). To solve this problem, I had, ironically, to refer to books and compilations written in the early twentieth century, when the memories of the characters of these books were still alive.

CHAPTER DESCRIPTIONS

The body of the book will be divided in two chapters. Chapter 2 studies the role of conservatism, the *Liberales Independientes* and their discourse of reasonability in the formation of a Panamanian political, proto-national and national identities in late nineteenth century Panama. It goes on to study periodicals, pamphlets and some literary works, to analyse the reception of conservatised-liberal and conservative ideas in the Panamanian press. The chapter shows the transformation of liberalism and sheds light on the legacies of *La Regeneración* in the building of the Panamanian national state.

Chapter 3 explains why Colombian and Panamanian conservative and moderate liberal intellectuals' rhetoric and policies promoted a kind of education that, allegedly, aimed as bringing up disciplined, methodical, objective and reasonable individuals. This education would compel them to seek the cosmopolitan reason and prevent struggle for political power. These arguments seemed consistent with the discourse of *La Regeneración*, appearing as essential to the projects of 'moral revolution' and 'scientific peace'. The chapter argues that as Christian morality, conservatism and science permeated the education system and went into schools, especially into teacher training schools, a conservative and moderate liberal pedagogical elite rose to reproduce the language, values, and practices of *La Regeneración*.

BIBLIOGRAPHY

Abel, Christopher. *Política, Iglesia y Partidos en Colombia 1886–1953* (Bogotá: FAES – Universidad de Colombia, 1987).

Anderson, Benedict. *Imagined Communites. Reflections on the Origin and Spread of Nationalism.* (London and New York: Verso, 2006).

Álvarez Gaviria, Jesús María and María Teresa Uribe de Hincapie. *Cien Años de Prensa en Colombia 1840–1940. Catálogo indizado de la prensa existente en la*

Sala de Periódicos de la Biblioteca Central de la Universidad de Antioquia. (Medellín: Imprenta Universidad de Antioquia, 2002).

Beluche, Olmedo. 'La separación de Panamá de Colombia. Mitos y Falsedades. Reflexiones sobre la Patria', in *Tareas* no. 122. (Panamá: Centro de Estudios Latinoamericanos "Justo Arosemena", Enero-Abril, 2006).

Beluche, Olmedo. *La verdadera historia de la separación de 1903: reflexiones en torno al centenario* (Panamá: Articsa, 2004).

Bernal, Juan Bosco. 'La Educación en Panamá: antecedentes, tendencias y perspectivas', *Panamá: Cien Años de República.* (Panamá: Manfer, S.A., 2004), pp. 47–76.

Bonilla, Heraclio et al. *Colombia y Panamá. Metamorfosis de una nación en el siglo XX.* Heraclio Bonilla and Gustavo Montañez, ed. (Bogotá: Universidad Nacional de Colombia, 2004).

Bourdieu, Pierre. *Capital cultural, escuela y espacio social.* Isabel Jiménez, trans. (Avellaneda, Argentina: Siglo Veintiuno Editores, S.A., 2008).

Bourdieu, Pierre. 'What Makes a Social Class? On The Theoretical and Practical Existence Of Groups' in *Berkeley Journal of Sociology*, Vol. 32 (Berkeley: Regents of the University of California: 1987), pp. 1–17. https://www.jstor.org/stable/41035356 Accessed: 19-02-2019.

Burke, Peter. *What is History of Knowledge?* (Cambridge: Polity Press, 2016).

Bushnell, David. *The Making of Modern Colombia. A nation in spite of itself* (Berkeley, Los Angeles, London: University of California Press, 1993).

Cabrera, Miguel Ángel. *Historia, Lenguaje y Teoría de la Sociedad.* (Valencia: Frónesis Cátedra Universitat de Valencia, 2001).

Caicedo, Rodolfo. 'Paz y Progreso (1904)' in *Revista Lotería* N° 60 (Panamá: May 1946), pp. 16–19.

Cantón, Alfredo. *Desenvolvimiento de las Ideas Pedagógicas en Panamá. 1903–1926.* (Panamá: Imprenta Nacional, 1955).

Castillero Calvo, Alfredo, 'El movimiento anseatista de 1826. La primera tentativa autonomista de istmeños después de la anexión a Colombia', *Tareas*, No. 4 (Panamá: Imprenta Panamá mayo-jul. 1961).

Céspedes Alemán, Francisco S. *La Educación en Panamá: panorama histórico y antología.* (Panamá: Imprenta Universitaria Biblioteca Cultural Panameña, 1981).

Conniff, Michael L. *Panama and the United States. The Forced Alliance* (Athens, Georgia; London: The University of Georgia Press, 1992).

Constitución de la República de Colombia de 1886. Edición Oficial (Bogotá: Imprenta de Vapor de Zalamea HS., 1886).

Culiolis, Andrés. *500 años de Educación en Panamá. Análisis crítico-político.* (Madrid and Panamá: Editora Escolar, S.A. – Susaeta Ediciones, S.A., 1992).

Davis, Harold Eugene. 'Jaime Balmes, Spanish Traditionalist: His Influence in Spanish America', *The Americas*, Vol. 35, No. 3 Academy of American

Franciscan History: January 1979), pp. 341–351. http://www.jstor.org/stable/980978

Del Cid Felipe, José Alberto. *Desarrollo de la Educación General y los inicios de la Universidad de Panamá.* (Panamá: Imprenta de la Universidad de Panamá, 2013).

Delpar, Helen. *Red Against Blue. The Liberal Party in Colombian Politics, 1863–1899.* (Alabama: The University of Alabama Press, 1981).

Díaz Espino, Ovidio. *El País creado por Wall Street. La historia prohibida de Panamá y su canal.* Trans. Angela García. (Barcelona: Ediciones Destino, S.A., 2004).

DuVal Jr., Miles. *From Cadiz to Cathay. The Story of the Long Diplomatic Struggle for the Panama Canal.* (Palo Alto: Stanford University Press, 1940).

Figueroa Navarro, Alfredo. *Dominio y Sociedad en el Panamá Colombiano (1821–1903)* (Panamá: Impresora Panamá, S.A., 1978).

Figueroa Navarro, Alfredo. 'El departamento de colombiano de Panamá a fines del siglo diecinueve e inicios de la vigésima centuria'. *Colombia y Panamá. Metamorfosis de una nación en el siglo XX.* Heraclio Bonilla and Gustavo Montañez, ed. (Bogotá: Universidad Nacional de Colombia, 2004), pp. 93–124.

Figueroa Navarro, Alfredo. *Grupos Populares de la Ciudad de Panamá,*

Franklin, Barry M., Pereyra Miguel A, Popkewitz, Thomas S. et al., *Cultural History and Education. Critical Essays on Knowledge and Schooling.* Barry M. Franklin, Miguel A. Pereyra, and Thomas S. Popkewitz eds. (New York: Routledgefalmer, 2001).

González Herrera, César Julio. *Aproximación Historiográfica al Pensamiento Ideológico-Político del Conservadurismo en Panamá,* (Panamá: Editorial Mariano Arosemena – Instituto Nacional de Cultura, 2003).

Gurdián Guerra, Reymundo. 'Entre luces y sombras: La enseñanza de las 'Historia de Panamá' y la Historiografía Republicana.' en *Historia General de Panamá.* Vol. III. Tomo II. Capítulo XVIII. Castillero Calvo, Alfredo (ed.) (Panamá: Comité del Centenario de la República, 2004), pp. 184–220.

Hale, Charles A. *La transformación del liberalismo en México a fines del siglo XIX.* (México: Fondo de Cultura Económica, 2002).

Hobsbawm, Eric. 'Inventing Traditions' in The Invention of Tradition, Eric Hobsbawm and Terence Ranger, eds. 20th printing (Cambridge: Cambridge University Press, 2012).

Informe que el Ministro de Instrucción Pública Presenten al Congreso de Colombia en sus sesiones de 1894. (Bogotá: Imprenta de la Luz, 1894).

Kirkendall, Andrew J.. 'Student Culture and Nation-State Formation' in *Beyond Imagined Communities. Reading and Writing the Nation in Nineteenth-Century Latin America.* John Charles Chasteen and Sara Castro-Klarén, eds.

(Washington, D.C., Baltimore and London: Woodrow Wilson Center Press – The Johns Hopkins University Press, 2003), pp. 84–111.

Kosselleck, Reinhart. *Futures Past. On the Semantics of Historical Time.* Keith Tribe, Trans. (New York: Columbia University Press, 2004). ·

Kosselleck, Reinhart. *The Practice of Conceptual History. Timing History, Spacing Concepts.* Todd Samuel Presner et al., trans. (Stanford: Stanford University Press, 2002).

Lasso, Marixa. Myths of Harmony. *Myths of Harmony: Race and Republicanism during the Age of Revolution, Colombia, 1795–1831.* (Pittsburgh: University of Pittsburgh Press, 2007).

Lemaitre, Eduardo., *Panamá y su separación de Colombia.* (Bogotá: Biblioteca Banco Popular – Editorial Kelly, 1971).

Mack, Gerstle. *The Land Divided. A history of the Panama Canal and Other Isthmian Canal Projects* (New York: Alfred A. Knopff, 1944).

Martínez Delgado, Luis. *Panamá: su independencia de España, su incorporación a la Gran Colombia, su separación de Colombia: el canal interoceánico.* (Bogotá: Ediciones Lerner, 1972).

McCullough, David. *The Path Between the Seas. The Creation of the Panama Canal. 1870–1914* (New York: Simon and Schuster, 1997).

McCain, William D. *The United States and the Republic of Panama* (Durham, North Carolina: Duke University Press, 1937).

Miller, Nicola. *In the Shadow of the State. Intellectuals and the Quest for National Identity in Twentieth-century Spanish America.* (London and New York: Verso, 1999).

Miller, Nicola. *Re-inventing Modernity in Latin America, 1900–1930.* (New York: Palgrave Macmillan, 2008).

Miró, Rodrigo. *Teoría de la Patria.*, En los quinientos años de la Nación Panameña en el Centenario de la República de Panamá. (Panamá: Sociedad Amigos de Panamá, 2003).

Molina Gerardo. *Las Ideas Liberales en Colombia – 1849–1914.* 4ta. Edición. (Bogotá: Ediciones Tercer Mundo, 1974).

Múñoz Pinzón, Armando. '*El Conflicto Azuereño de 1854*' in *Historia General de Panamá.* Vol. II. Tomo III. Capítulo V. Castillero Calvo, Alfredo (ed.) (Panamá: Comité del Centenario de la República, 2004), 176–192,

Palacios, Marco. *Between Legitimacy and Violence. A History of Colombia, 1875–2002.* (Durham and London: Duke University Press, 2006).

Palacios, Marco and Frank Safford. *Colombia: Fragmented Land, Divided Society* (New York: Oxford University Press, 2001).

Park, James W. *Rafael Núñez and the Politics of Colombian Regionalism, 1863–1886.* (Baton Rouge and London: Louisiana State University Press, 1985).

Popkewitz, Thomas S. *Cosmopolitanism and the Age of School Reform. Science, Education, and the Making of the Child.* (New York: Routledge, 2008).

Posada-Carbó, Eduardo. 'Limits of Power: Elections under the Conservative Hegemony in Colombia, 1886–1930', *The Hispanic American Historical Review*, Vol. 77, N° 2 (Durham: Duke University Press, 1997), pp. 245–279. http://www.jstor.org/2516902.

Revista Lotería N° 60 (Panamá: Mayo de 1946).

Safford, Frank *The Ideal of the Practical. Colombia's Struggle to Form a Technical Elite*. (Austin and London: University of Texas Press, 1976).

Smith, Anthony. *Nationalism. Theory, Ideology, History*. (Cambridge and Massachusetts: Polity Press, 2008).

Soler, Ricaurte. *El Pensamiento político en los siglos XIX y XX* (Panamá: Universidad de Panamá, 1988).

Soler, Ricaurte. ed. *Pensamiento Panameño y Concepción de la Nacionalidad durante el siglo XIX* (para la historia de las ideas en el Istmo). 2da. Edición. (Panamá: Librería Cultural Panameña, S.A., 1971).

Soler, Ricaurte. *Formas Ideológicas de la Nación Panameña* (Panamá: Ediciones de la Revista "Tareas", 1963).

Soler, Ricaurte. Panamá: Oligarquía y Nación, 1925–1972. (Panamá: Ediciones de la *Revista Tareas*, 1976).

Valenzuela, J. Samuel 'Class Relations and Democratization. A reassessment of Barrington Moore's Model', Miguel Ángel Centeno and Fernando López-Alves, ed. *The Other Mirror. Grand Theory Through The Lens of Latin America*. (Princeton and Oxford: Princeton University Press, 2001).

Zea, Leopoldo. *El positivismo en México: Nacimiento, apogeo y decacencia.* (México: Fondo de Cultura Económica, 1968).

CHAPTER 2

La Regeneración and Paz Científica in Colombian Panama, 1878–1903

On 24 May 1884, *El Istmeño*, the official newspaper of the Conservative Party in Panama, exhibited the motto 'God, Fatherland and Freedom' as part of its headers. The phrase could be interpreted to mean that belief in God was more important than faithfulness to Colombia and Panama and the will to be free. It also implied that the Catholic religion was necessary to achieve and maintain freedom in the Fatherland. This short-lived Conservative newspaper published an announcement for the Colombian national electoral campaign and local elections. The writers highlighted their support for the candidacy of prominent liberal intellectual and politician, Dr Justo Arosemena.[1] In the editorial article, *El Istmeño* stated that since the civil war of 1876–1877, the Conservative Party had fought to reform the federalist Constitution of 1863. It added that many liberals had slowly begun to join the call for reformation; 'although late', the newspapers said 'the [Liberal Party] sings a palinody'.[2] It provided examples of how two Liberal newspapers, *La Luz*, a supporter of the *Liberales Independientes* and *Diario de Cundinamarca*, a publication of the *Liberales Radicales*, had requested constitutional reform. In addition, El Istmeño, indicated that 'a Liberal with honourable purposes, recognised the flaws of the Constitution of 1863 and demanded its reform. That patriot was Mister

---

[1] Editorial. 'Cuestión Capital', *El Istmeño*. Año II. Serie IV. Número 19. (Panamá: 24 May 1884), p. 1.
[2] Ibid.

© The Author(s) 2020
R. de la Guardia Wald, *Education, Conservatism, and the Rise of a Pedagogical Elite in Colombian Panama*,
https://doi.org/10.1007/978-3-030-50046-7_2

41

Justo Arosemena.' After stating that he was the candidate selected by the Isthmian Conservative Party to 'rule the destiny of this state',[3] *El Istmeño* explained that Justo Arosemena had 'presented [in *La Luz*] a study of the [Constitution of 1863] together with a reform project … that adapts to the current necessities of the Republic [i.e., Estados Unidos de Colombia]'.[4] A connoted advocate of liberalism and as a *Liberal Radical*, this alliance with Miguel Antonio Caro and Rafael Núñez might seem strange to many readers today, especially because Justo Arosemena was himself one of the elaborators of the Constitution of 1863. Moreover, Núñez, Caro and *La Regeneración* have been portrayed as oppressive for Panamanian Liberals in most Isthmian nationalist historiography. The example of Justo Arosemena, though, reflects the conservatisation of liberalism that was happening in Colombia, Panama and other parts of the Americas at the time. The fact that *El Istmeño* referred to Liberal newspapers also illustrates a liberalisation of conservatism. These transformations were symptomatic of the way conservatives and sometimes liberals interpreted the political experiences that resulted from the creation of the Constitution of 1863. By the 1880s, some conservative and liberal reformers criticised the implausibility of reforming the Constitution and argued that the way it was designed implied that it was infallible.

Following this line of thought, *El Istmeño* made an analysis of the articles published in *La Luz* and the *Diario de Cundinamarca*. The main object of the text was to demonstrate that there was a consensus in the questioning of Article 92 of the Constitution of 1863, which stipulated the steps and requirements for a partial or full reform to occur. First of all, any reform had to be requested as voted by a majority in all states. Second, the reform had to be discussed and approved by both the Senate and Congress. Third, the reform had to be ratified by all the plenipotentiaries or representatives of each state. Alternatively, the Constitution could be reformed if Congress called for a Convention, but it had to be demanded unanimously by the legislatives bodies of all the states.[5] *El Istmeño* goes on to disapprove the *Liberales Radicales'* rejection of any amendment to the document, stating:

[3] Ibid.
[4] Ibid.
[5] Ministerio Ejecutivo de los Estados Unidos de Colombia. 'Cápitulo XII, Articulo 92' in *Constitución política de los Estados Unidos de Colombia de 1863*. (Colombia: 8 de Mayo de 1863) Accessed: http://www.cervantesvirtual.com/obra-visor/colombia-29/html/02613e70-82b2-11df-acc7-002185ce6064_1.html#I_23_

If the Liberal Party believes it is the driving force behind republican progress, how can it oppose the reform [of the Constitution of 1863]? ... This party battles against the infallibility of the Holy Church, but it considers itself infallible? As we advance in our republican life we have new needs that must be satisfied.[6]

Implicitly, *El Istmeño*'s editors viewed the rejection of reform as arrogant, autocratic or unreasonable: if the Pope's divine authority was challengeable, then the authority of the *Liberales Radicales* could be too. As in other parts of Colombia, the transformation of liberalism and conservatism was the result of the re-evaluation that some intellectuals made of the past–present. For them, to become or remain modern, intellectuals, politicians and the population in general needed to acknowledge that 'new needs' had surpassed those of the past.

Part I. The Foundations of *La Regeneración*: Sociology for *Paz Científica*

Drawing upon Charles Hale's study on Mexico, this book posits that an evolution of liberalism was also occurring in Colombia when Rafael Núñez proposed a political regeneration. In 'La Paz Científica', an article written in 1882, Núñez postulated that Liberal dogmatism was unsustainable because it caused the exclusion of the opposition, a grave mistake.[7] Five major problems derived from this exclusion: first, the state bureaucracy and services lacked effectiveness because workers did not possess the required skill sets to carry out administrative tasks. Second, the intellectual benefits of ideological competition were lost. Third, political exclusion permitted an oligarchic system of governance that undermined the fundamental principles of the constitution. Fourth, this 'illegitimate' oligarchic system of governance had not only become corrupt, but also emanated injustice spreading it to the wider society. Fifth, a lack of external competition caused quarrels within the Liberal Party. He claimed that under these circumstances 'a spark is enough to produce an explosion'.[8] Núñez stated

---

[6] Editorial. 'Cuestión Capital', *El Istmeño* ... p. 1.
[7] Rafael Núñez. 'La Paz Científica', *La Reforma Política* ... (Bogotá: no publisher indicated, 1888), p. 100.
[8] Ibid., p. 101.

that, in order to avoid revolt, the Liberal Party needed to restructure and seek unification in the true practice of its beliefs. He added that 'the attraction of ideas can only unite men, when … the magnet of material benefit disappears'.[9] A moral introspection was needed to achieve this reorganisation, since material and political ambition had distorted and weakened the Liberal Party's aims and ideals.

Moreover, he claimed that Conservatives were aware of the need to prevent intransigency. Núñez contended that *Liberales Independientes* and Conservatives were ready to replace intolerance as they were both 'tired of violence'.[10] Núñez argued that politics was an experimental science, which served to find a practical solution to prevent conflicts.[11] After empirical and historical analyses of Colombia's constitutions, he determined that only the 'strictly authoritarian' constitution of 1843 had guaranteed a period of public order.[12] To justify such a proposal, he exalted the Napoleonic French Empire, because it ended the 'terrible carnival of bloodshed' that followed the French Revolution.[13] Thus, he defended that a practical solution was needed and that the best way to avoid conflict was to return to an authoritarian and centralist political system.[14]

Núñez was also was an admirer of positivists like Herbert Spencer and John Stuart Mill[15] and of the positivist *Reforma* in Mexico.[16] Following these models, he implemented policies that were supposedly based on his sociological analysis of Colombian political history and cultural qualities. His observations led to the conclusion that progress was not only about scientific knowledge, but also about enhancing morality or civic virtues. Accordingly, the latter must be informed by an indispensable spiritual element. Although this might suggest that Núñez was adopting Comte's 'Religion of Humanity',[17] as did many of his contemporaries in Mexico, he explicitly said that Spencer was the 'most advanced … exponent, and true

[9] Ibid., p. 102.
[10] Ibid, p. 103.
[11] Ibid., p. 100.
[12] Ibid., pp. 98–100.
[13] Ibid., p. 103.
[14] Ibid., p. 104.
[15] Ferro Bayón, p. 224.
[16] Rafael Núñez. 'La lección de México', *La Reforma Política en Colombia*. Tomo VI. (Bogotá: Editorial A B C – Biblioteca Popular de Cultura Colombiana, 1945), p. 15.
[17] See: William D. Raat. 'Agustín Aragón and México's Religion of Humanity', *Journal of Inter-American Studies*, Vol. 11. No. 3. (Miami: Center for Latin American Studies at the University of Miami, July, 1969), pp. 441–457.

founder of the new science [of sociology]'.[18] His predilection was detailed in 'La Sociología':

> Comte considers a subjective analysis of our ideas to be impossible, while Spencer supports the belief in the subjective science of the spirit ... Although [Comte] recognises the necessity of religion, he claims that the human genre itself is the ... object for that religion. In Comte's system, humanity is the superior being, whereas Spencer recognises that religion constitutes an omniscient force that we must seek to understand ... Comte's system intends ... to absorb all individual forces, but Spencer's [system] leads to the complete opposite. There might be a sentimental harmony, but [it would be] a free harmony, as a result ... of moral progress. Spencer believes that the final destiny of man is total morality.[19]

Núñez sustained that analysing the spiritual aspects of a human being and humanity in general was necessary to understand and guide religion. However, a creed should not establish a cult to human beings, but to look for an ulterior purpose beyond material life. When all humans, individually, join in harmony they will reach perfection or 'total morality'. In short, adding a spiritual aspect to the scientific study of society will help the whole of humanity to unite under a moral ideal of progress.

In this text, Núñez also intended to foment the study of sociology. He confessed that, initially, he did not understand social science because his generation was educated under the influence of the French Enlightenment and passionate republicanism. His contemporaries understood that the republican system was the paradigm of 'liberty and justice'.[20] Núñez claimed that later he discovered that it could be tyrannical too.[21] Although recognising that *Liberales Radicales* had a 'period of splendour', which served Colombian society well, he was of the opinion that this political school had become too dogmatic and intolerant.[22] Núñez argued that the leaders of the Liberal Party began to create laws based on 'retrograde teachings' fed in part by federalism and the complete freedom of press established in the Constitution of 1863.[23] These, he claimed, led to

---

[18] Rafael Núñez. 'La Sociología', *La Reforma Política en Colombia*. (Bogotá: no information, 1888), p. 393. The article was published in 1883.
[19] Ibid., pp. 402–403.
[20] Ibid., p. 393.
[21] Ibid., pp. 393–394.
[22] Ibid., p 414.
[23] Ibid., p. 415.

rhetorical talk about political liberty, freedom of thought and republican-ism, but, in reality, their 'deeds did not match their bold words'.[24] For him, the lack of consistency between discourse and practice was one of the main causes of continuous conflict between 1863 and 1880.

After a reinterpretation of readings on sociology, Núñez affirmed that he learned how to truly structure a republican political government. He concluded that the 'laws of social dynamics' require 'coexistence of oppos-ing factors' as the source for equilibrium and peace.[25] For achieve peaceful coexistence, it was necessary to understand the sociological nature of the governed country: political leaders had to contemplate the cultural and spiritual character of the population before creating any policy or reform.[26] Accordingly, the nature of Colombian society was connected to Hispanic traditions and Christianity, so Catholicism needed to be protected and promoted to achieve moral rejuvenation.[27] His reform, then, promoted both an ethnic and a civic nationalism. It was ethnic in the sense that it included the cultural element of religion; it was civic, for the instillment of Catholic morality aimed at consolidating respect for the law, social order and peace.

PART II. THE 'MORAL REVOLUTION' OF RAFAEL NÚÑEZ AND MIGUEL ANTONIO CARO

From all the Conservative ideologues Rafael Núñez found his closest ally in Miguel Antonio Caro, a vehement defender of Catholicism and the Spanish language as a symbol of the Colombian nation and as sources of order and discipline.[28] This Conservative leader shared Núñez's rejection of the *Liberales Radicales'* utilitarianism and the conviction that moral restructuring was needed to save Colombia from catastrophe. In spite of his Conservative ideology, Caro's political and philosophical discourse resembled some of Núñez's positivist ideas.

For instance, in Caro's 'Historia y Filosofía' (History and Philosophy), an article written in 1882, Caro defended Núñez's first presidency after

[24] Ibid., p. 414.
[25] Ibid., p. 415.
[26] Ibid., pp. 399–401.
[27] Ibid., p. 399.
[28] Malcolm Deas. 'Miguel Antonio Caro y amigos: Gramática y Poder en Colombia', *Del Poder y la Gramática y otros ensayos sobre historia, política y literatura colombianas.* (Bogotá: Tercer Mundo Editores, 1993), pp. 47–49.

the latter received criticism from the *Liberales Radicales.* They had accused Núñez of attempting to monopolise power[29] and provoking war.[30] But Caro defended that he had opted to divide the Liberal Party, instead of remaining as a part of a forced Liberal alliance.[31] Caro indicated that such an alliance between *Liberales Radicales* and *Independientes* was contrary to 'the logic of events ...'; it was a union that 'God did not bless'.[32] Their division was inevitable as 'the decomposition of expiring beings' from which 'new organisms [were] produced'.[33] Finally, he praised the project of *La Regeneración* because it promoted tolerance and sought for 'equilibrium'.[34] Caro said that:

> Militant parties ... necessitate civil war or despotism ... But such a violent state cannot subsist indefinitely in a progressive society. In a republic, it is necessary to search for a middle ground that ensures order and consolidates peace in institutions in which the party has no vested interest ... as a genuine expression of common need ... There is something that parties must recognize and respect: the fatherland.[35]

Caro's discourse combined ideas from positivism and a Catholic belief in resurrection to describe the ending of a social system and the coming of a new one. He concurred with Núñez that there were historical processes that should ultimately give birth to a new positive era. This required the transformation of Colombian liberalism, a process that depended on the philosophical and political actions of the *Liberales Independientes.*

His words implied that the transformation of political parties and the search for consensus were a patriotic deeds, because these prevented violence and helped establish proper republican institutions. Caro proposed the reformation of the *Constitución de Río Negro*, the allegedly legal bastion of the *Liberales Radicales.* He argued that this constitution had two major flaws: intolerance of conservatism and 'malevolence' against Catholicism. These defects deprived many citizens of an egalitarian and impartial code of law. Furthermore, Caro criticised the conflict resulting from what he called the three absolute freedoms or 'sovereignties' granted

---

[29] Miguel Antonio Caro. 'Historia y Filosofía', *Escritos Políticos.* Carlos Valderrama Andrade, comp. (Bogotá: Fundación Caro y Cuervo, 1990), p. 34. Published in 1882.

[30] Ibid., p. 38.

[31] Ibid., p. 41.

[32] Ibid., pp. 40–41.

[33] Ibid., p. 41.

[34] Ibid., p. 42.

[35] Ibid., p. 33.

in the Constitution of 1863. He categorised the three freedoms as individual, provincial and national. He explained that individual sovereignty allowed for tyranny and injustice; provincial sovereignty made the Constitution 'impractical' because of its excessive federalism. His argument pointed to the belief that national sovereignty had great limitations, as the constitution was arbitrarily inclined to favour one of the two other kinds of 'sovereignties'.[36] In other words, he deemed these absolute freedoms to be a trigger of turmoil because the freedom of an individual, of the local government and of the national government did not always share the same interests. Moreover, Caro claimed that 'total [individual] freedom ... entails the decentralization of censorship'.[37] He claimed that the creators of the *Constitución de Río Negro* had been too lenient.[38] He conveyed that, to truly establish social order in Colombia, there needed to be an authority to mediate between the freedom of the individual, the provinces, and the national government.[39] For Caro, as for Núñez, a fairly authoritarian government was a prerequisite for administering justice and controlling freedom efficiently. This is why the motto of the conservatives at the time was '*in justitia libertas*' or 'liberty within justice': the right to justice was more important than the right to freedom.

Furthemore, in 'Libertad Radical' (or the freedom of the *Liberales Radicales*), he argued that if the regeneration of the *Liberales Independientes* was to happen and have a legacy, it needed to fight the doctrine of the *Liberales Radicales* and to change the culture of Colombian justice and legislation.[40] In order to explain the problem of moral decay, he argued that it was necessary to make a distinction between 'legal freedom' and 'moral freedom'. An individual or a collective could live without punishment if their actions complied with the law, but this was not necessarily true in the realm of morality. Then, he claimed that many *Liberales Radicales* considered that 'legal freedom equates moral freedom', leading them to confuse everything that the law tolerates or everything that is deemed as legal with what is moral. According to Caro, this was a mistake produced by utilitarianism's neglect of natural law, rejecting the idea that human beings have inherent and inalienable

---

[36] Ibid., p. 34.
[37] Miguel Antonio Caro. 'Libertad Radical', *Escritos Políticos* ..., p. 28
[38] Ibid., p.27.
[39] Ibid.
[40] Ibid., p. 32.

rights. Besides this, *Liberales Radicales* practiced an 'impious repudiation of positive religion'.[41] In order to base legal freedom on morality, utilitarianism and *radicalismo* had to give way to a moral political system which based its policy-making on religious values.

The approximation to Caro and the combination of positivism and Catholicism was corroborated by Núñez in 'Revolución Moral'. An apparently elated Núñez celebrated Caro's argument that the new constitution had indeed set the basis for a 'moral revolution'.[42] He argued that favouring religious policies was acceptable, for this 'religious reaction' was a 'a moral reaction'.[43] Albeit he still deemed these policies as based in empirical knowledge and coherent with the positivist goal of consolidating *Paz Científica*. In his words, '*La Regeneración* is not calculation, but faith.'[44] In other words, progress could not be achieved only through scientific calculations and predictions; the regeneration needed a moral aspect and true believers to materialise the expectations of establishing order and reaching a better life.

PART III. NEGOTIATING *LA REGENERACIÓN* IN PANAMA, 1878–1903

To promote *La Regeneración* in Panama, Núñez and his followers attempted to show the reform complied with the aspirations of order of the Isthmus' population. In 1879, Rafael Núñez wrote an article that analysed the problems of the *Estado Soberano de Panamá*. He criticised *Liberales Radicales* leaders like Rafael Aizpuru for trying to take control of the Panamanian *cacicazgo* (chiefdom). Núñez posited that their cause was unpopular in Panama, because Isthmians were looking for something new. He claimed that Panamanian society had experienced constant turmoil, so now it had a 'regenerative fever' or a desire for regeneration.[45] Although Núñez had detractors in Panama, the evidence suggests that *La Regeneración* had more advocates in the Isthmus than is assumed in conventional historiography.

---

[41] Ibid., p. 27.
[42] Rafael Núñez. 'Revolución Moral', *La Reforma Política*. Tomo II. (Bogotá: Editorial A B C – Biblioteca Popular de Cultura Colombiana, 1945), p. 353.
[43] Ibid., p. 358.
[44] Ibid., pp. 353–360.
[45] Rafael Núñez. 'La Situación', *La Reforma Política en Colombia*. Tomo II...., p. 101.

It is plausible that many Panamanians supported Núñez for his close connections with the Isthmus and with important Panamanian leaders. In fact, Núñez's first governmental position was that of Judge of the District of Chiriquí.[46] He also married the sister-in-law of José de Obaldía (1806–1889),[47] one of the most prominent landowners in Chiriquí, who became President of Colombia (1854–1855). In 1858, José de Obaldía won the elections for Governor and named Núñez Vice-Governor of the Isthmus. De Obaldía was absent the day he was supposed to take office, so Núñez became temporary Governor of Panama in 1858. In addition, Núñez was elected to be Senator for the State of Panama in 1860.[48] It is also important to say that Núñez was from Cartagena, so he presented himself as an advocate of the regional interests of the *Costa* (the Caribbean coastal region of Colombia).[49] The extent to which Isthmians received and supported *La Regereneración* varied depending on their political affiliation, and on how political experiences fulfilled expectations. In any case, their descriptions of events presented in newspapers, pamphlets and others spaces illustrate the process of construction of Panamanian political and proto-national identities.

The Transformation of Liberalism in the Isthmus

As in the case of Justo Arosemena, at the end of the nineteenth century many Isthmian Liberals, including *Liberales Radicales* and critics of Núñez, displayed similar language and practices to that of their alleged political adversaries. This contained positivist, moralist and religious messages. This was the result of a transformation of liberalism, a process of conservatisation. For instance, Isthmian moderate liberals, who were not adepts of the *Liberales Independientes*, were not all receptive to the views of *La Regeneración*. Actually, at the end of the 1870s, many Panamanian Liberals and Conservatives distrusted Núñez's proposal for political reform.

In this sense, it is worth mentioning *El Precursor*, a newspaper founded in 1878 by journalist and lawyer, M. R. de la Torre and Ignacio de la Torre. Although M. R. de la Torre was a liberal, he stated that *El Precursor*

---

[46] Park, p. 76.
[47] Aparicio, p. 237.
[48] Ibid., p. 246.
[49] Park, p. 76.

did not favour either Liberals or Conservatives. Instead, he proposed to publish a newspaper that did not have a political line but a 'social creed' that could be summarized in five concepts: tolerance, liberty, equality, fraternity and democracy. Following the spirit of these words, he invited a conservative, Tomás Casís,[50] to join him as editor of *El Precursor*.[51] In the first editorial of *El Precursor*, de la Torre emphasized the importance of tolerance, saying it was one of the most essential virtues of a 'loyal and free republican ... [and] the foundation of the freedom of thought'. He claimed that eradication of intolerance was necessary because Colombia was passing through a 'political tempest'. Therefore, 'only with tolerance can we achieve salvation'.[52] In spite of the similar rhetoric imbued in de la Torre's 'social creed' and that of Núñez's regeneration (in the sense that both pointed out tolerance as necessary for 'saving the nation' and reaching social order), de la Torre was not a partisan of *La Regeneración*.[53]

Later, de la Torre apparently abandoned the periodical. But, whether for profit or true tolerance, his next publishing endeavours showed a transformation: he began printing newspapers for the *Conservadores Históricos*, such as *El Sufragio*, and *El Fiscón Impertinente* and *El Constitucional* for the *Liberales Independientes*. He also published the works of conservative intellectuals like Manuel José Pérez and Colombian pedagogue Manuel Dávila Flórez.[54]

[50] He followed de la Torre's view in Tomás Casís. '¿Con quién debe el Partido Conservador hacer la liga?', *El Precursor*. Trimestre VI. N° 66. Panamá: 12 de julio de 1879. Later, he also evolved as seen in Tomás Casís. 'Speech during Homenaje al Sr. Quijano Otero', *El Precursor*. Año III. Trimestre XI. N° 130. Panamá: 25 de octubre de 1880, p. 1.

[51] On many occasions either De la Torre or Casís occupied the position of sole editor. From the sources obtained in the National Library in Colombia, Casís was the sole editor of this newspaper for the first time from 31 August 1878 to 7 September 1878, and for the second time from 5 October 1878 to at least 25 October 1880. It is during this last period, specifically on the 12 July 1879, that *El Precursor* defined itself as the 'Official Organ of the Conservative Party of the Isthmus'.

[52] M. R De la Torre. 'Nuestro Programa', *El Precursor*. Trimestre I. N° 1. Panamá: Imprenta de M. R. de la Torre e Hijos, 24 de febrero de 1878, p. 1

[53] For more examples see: M. R. de la Torre. 'Calaverada insigne', *El Precursor*. Trimestre I. N° 11. Panamá: Imprenta de M. R. de la Torre e Hijos, 9 de mayo de 1878, p. 1

[54] Manuel Dávila Florez was a conservative pedagogue and intellectual from Mompox, and would-be Secretary of Public Instruction of Colombia. His *Cartas de Instrucción Pública* was published in Panamá by de la Torre. See: Manuel Dávila Florez. *Cartas de Instrucción Pública* (Panamá: Tipografía M. R. de la Torres, 1893). (Panamá: Tipografía M. R. de la Torre, 1893).

Nevertheless, sometimes, he also published the works of *Liberales Radicales* such as Belisario Porras.[55]

Possibly, the most significant example of the conservatisation of liberalism in Panama is that of would-be President of Panama (1910–1912), Pablo Arosemena. At the start of the *La Regeneración*, he was a supporter of Núñez, having been chosen as a candidate to the Presidency of the Estado de Panamá for the period between 1882 and 1884 by the *Liberales Independientes* of the Isthmus. This candidacy was announced in *El Derecho*, 'Official instrument of the [*Liberal*] *Independiente* directory of the State [of Panama]', which transcribed a speech by the Director of the Escuela Normal de Varones, Adolfo Fernández, who described Arosemena as 'apostle and martyr of *La Regeneración*'.[56] Besides the speech, this newspaper published an article that affirmed that:

> The programme proposed by [Rafael Núñez] includes parts of our political aspirations. The moment has come … in which, tired of constant fighting, we are yearning for peace … Moderation and tolerance with our opponents is the [political] line of *El Derecho*.[57]

Panamanian *Liberales Independientes* not only viewed Núñez as a political representative of their party, they allegedly supported *La Regeneración*'s tolerance of their rivals as a way to finally consolidate peace. Despite this initial support for Núñez's campaign, Arosemena abandoned *La Regeneración* in 1882. The conflict between both politicians had many personal and political motivations. One of them was that, as official candidate of the *Liberales Independientes* in the Isthmus, Arosemena and his followers expected the backing of Núñez. This political support never materialised, because Núñez he decided that the current President of the State of Panama, Dámaso Cervera, would continue in his position. This

[55] Belisario Porras. *Galimatías o Marsías tocando la flauta*. (Panamá: Imprenta de M. R. de la Torre e Hijos, 1891)

[56] Adolfo Fernández. 'Discurso pronunciado por el señor Adolfo Fernández en el banquete que los miembros del Partido Independiente de la ciudad de Panamá dieron al señor doctor Ricardo Becerra, el 12 de diciembre de 1880, en el "Jardín del Paraíso"', *El Derecho*. Año I. Serie I. N° 2, Panamá, 25 de enero de 1881, p. 1.

[57] Editorial. 'Una vez por todas', *El Derecho*. Año I. Serie I. N° 2, Panamá, 25 de enero de 1881, p. 1.

caused friction between Arosemena and Núñez.[58] The two politicians engaged in a diatribe that reflected in several writings, even after the latter's death in 1894.[59]

After 1903, Arosemena still notionally followed the precepts of a conservatised-liberalism. In his 'Declaración del 4 de noviembre de 1903' (Declaration of 4 November 1903), which described his vision for Panama's future after its secession from Colombia, Arosemena confessed that Panama was not yet ready for independence because the Isthmus had not attained the moral and material resources to survive as a 'serious political organization'.[60] He recommended that if Panama did not want to become a mere outlier territory, it needed to understand the gravity of the situation. He wrote:

> Mr. Thiers, the founder of the French Republic once said: 'The Republic will be Conservative or it will not be'. Inspired by such a learned man, I say: 'The Republic of Panama will be organized and peaceful, or it will not be' ... Only an organised and successful Republic of Panama will justify the events of 3 November 1903. It is fair to recognize and proclaim ... [that] the dividing line between parties has been erased and that there are only Isthmians ... working to establish a regime of integrity, law and justice; and to found, with moral peace, healthy governance and an immutable rule of the law.[61]

The notion of *Paz Científica* as being necessary to orientate a path of peace and prosperity is self-evident from this quotation. The use of concepts like 'organised' country, 'moral peace' and 'integrity, law and justice' are not dissimilar to the ideals of 'moral renovation' and 'liberty within justice'. The celebration of tolerance between the political parties also shows incorporation of the rhetoric of *La Regeneración*. Pablo Arosemena's

---

[58] Enrique Arce and Juan. B. Sosa. Compendio de Historia de Panamá: Texto adoptado oficialmente para la enseñanza en las escuelas y colegios de la nación (Panamá: Casa Editorial del 'Diario de Panamá', 1911), pp. 270–273.

[59] Rafael Núñez quoted in Pablo Arosemena. 'El cordero de Cartagena', *Escritos.* Tomo I. (Panamá: Imprenta Nacional, 1930); Pablo Arosemena. 'La conversión del señor Núñez', *Escritos.* Tomo I. (Panamá: Imprenta Nacional, 1930); Pablo Arosemena. *El Derrumbe de una Leyenda*, Biblioteca Cultural Nacional. Serie 2. N° 24. Guillermo Andreve, ed. (Panamá: Tipografía Moderna, noviembre, 1918).

[60] Pablo Arosemena. 'La declaración del 4 de noviembre de 1903', *Escritos.* (Panamá: Imprenta Nacional, 1930), p. 147.

[61] Ibid., 148.

words are not only a call for an ordered and peaceful republic, but also a plea to abandon the Colombian past. The rejection of such a period of crisis, disorder and violence which impeded Panama from being organised and successful would be the best justification for secession. The fact that a strong critic of Núñez adapted his language and elaborated a similar horizon of expectations suggests that such a discourse also appealed some other Liberal politicians and intellectuals in Panama before and after the time of Independence in 1903.

More evidence of the liberals becoming conservatised is an article published in *El Aspirante*, a *Liberal Radical* newspaper: '*Razón, Justicia y Buena Fe*' ('Reason, Justice and Good Faith'). Its writer defended the ideas of Catalan priest Jaume Balmes (1810–1848) to whom the article attributes a positivist vision of society, by presenting his ideas as following the stages model similar to those of Comte. The author explained that Balmes had inspired 'excellent and beneficial governmental' policies that would bring 'peace between those governed though a profoundly moral medium, that would also serve to strengthen those in power'. The writer concluded that it was important to distrust the

> promises and advice of intransigent parties, whether in politics or in social life, for they obligate to act against reason, [and] to wrench the wand of justice. If in purity can there be government; if we shall have a democratic nation, it is necessary to fix everything, harmonise everything, [and] see how [opposing parties] achieve peace … without clashes and tearing themselves to pieces … We must find a common middle ground that combines the necessities of civil life with good political practice … The Government of Colombia needs to inspire … a trust that can only be obtained by those who work towards … social peace![62]

The author defends the harmonising of politics, moderation and peaceful co-existence. Although not using the exact same words as *Liberales Independientes* and Conservatives, with its talk of purity and harmony, '*Razón, Justicia y Buena Fe*' seems to have adopted a religious vernacular. From the mere fact that the author is referring to a Catholic philosoper, it is possible to infer that the 'moral medium' could be religion or, at least a source of moral thinking, as the means to 'fix' or regenerate

---

[62] 'Razón, Justicia y Buena Fe', *El Aspirante*. Año II. N° 64: 2 de abril de 1892, p. 2

everything. This was mandatory to instaurate the more stable kind of peace: 'social peace'. This rhetoric recalls the discourse promoting *Paz Científica*, and the moral revolution of *La Regeneración*.

La Regeneración *in Panamanian Conservative and* Liberal Independiente *Newspapers*

Support for Nuñez's political reform is visible in at least twenty-five *Independiente* and Conservative periodicals that appeared in Panama between 1878 and 1903.[63] Amidst political strife, the two political factions in the Isthmus discursively promoted the roll-out of the *Paz Científica* through social order, tolerance and morality. This can be seen in the messages comprised and constantly repeated in their newspapers and pamphlets.

There is some evidence that not only liberalism evolved, but also conservatism. Let us take the example of M. R. de la Torre's conservative colleague, Tomás Casís, who was not initially a supporter of Núñez's political reform. His initial sceptical disposition towards *La Regeneración* seemed to dissipate when Rafael Núñez became President in 1880. Tomás Casís' new attitude can be perceived in a letter published in his newspaper, *El Precursor*, which welcomed Núñez during his visit to Panama. The letter congratulated the new President, wished for a prosperous Colombia and hoped for a 'renovation of party culture and our government's enlightening and morality', so that Colombia could 'fulfil its destiny in the midst of peace and unity'.[64] The example illustrates the change of adhesions to political parties or to political characters. Casís publicly supported the idea that tolerance between parties and moral governance were elements necessary to achieve peace. He tried to rally support for *La Regeneración*.

Defence for the policies of Núñez and Caro continued in Panama after the creation of the Constitution of 1886. In 1891, another article published in a *Liberal Independiente* newspaper, *El Aliento*, applauded *La Regeneración*'s laws regarding censorship, centralisation and the death penalty. The article claimed, for example, that regulations limited abuses previously committed by and in the Colombian press. Yet it also argued

---

[63] This is the number of newspapers the researcher found in the newspaper collection of the Biblioteca Nacional de Colombia and Biblioteca Luis Ángel Arango.

[64] Tomás Casís. 'Nuestra Felicitación al Ciudadano Presidente de la República', in *El Precursor*. Año III. Trimestre XI. N° 130. Panamá: 25 de octubre de 1880, p. 3.

that the censorship law still offered plenty of space for freedom of thought. According to the article, these limitations served for the moral and material growth of the nation. In addition, it questioned the critics of such laws by asking them if there could ever be progress when the press 'works as a torch that nurtures the flame of discord'. Furthermore, the article also affirmed it was better to restrict what was published in the press than to appear hypocritical by boasting about unlimited freedoms without complying with them to the extent of causing turmoil and even potential civil war.[65] Moreover, it emphasised the point that restraining the old tendencies of the Colombian press brought a period of intellectual and material development to the nation.[66] As can be observed, the *Liberales Independientes'* press viewed the control of the freedom of opinion as a way to stop defamation and fake news, and to impede intellectual regress. Intrinsically, *El Aliento* posited that the information could not be speculative and lacking in evidence, but had to be objective and even scientific. Putting controls on misinformation and calumny was a route to a more civilised form of political debate.

The Conservative and *Liberal Independiente* idea of what kind of development this new press law brought can be noticed in an article written for the *Liberal Independiente* the newspaper, *El Constitucional,* which argued that since freedom of the press was officially regulated no disturbance had occurred in Colombia, because 'opinions … [are manifested] frankly but respectfully by means of a press that … [does] its rightful task: to civilize the masses'. Debate in the press, it indicated, is beneficial for the development of ideas and for the promotion and practice of 'good habits'.[67] In other words, proper discussion in the media was a civilising act, because it educated the population. In addition, the idea that one of the goals of the Conservative and *Liberal Independiente* press was to promote that practice and sustainability of 'good habits' is related to Núñez's and Caro's programme for spreading 'moral renovation'.

More accessible newspapers tried to show Panamanian readers some of Núñez's positivist philosophy in an amenable manner. In 1887, *El Fiscón Impertinente* published some of his poems such as 'Lo Invisible.' This poem reads:

[65] Editorial. 'Se amostazan', in *El Aliento*. Panamá: 30 de enero de 1891, pp. 1–2.
[66] Ibid.
[67] Publícola (pen name of anonymous). 'El Partido Independiente o Nacional', *El Constitucional*. Panamá: 1 de febrero de 1891, pp. 2–3.

There is a world without boundaries, ineffable
Moral World, immense, immeasurable
Where there should be no boundaries no mistakes ...

Man always walks towards that world
And what once was in the offing
Today is, already, a centre occupied by his sprouts,
Because of this, his [i.e. humans'] being improves more and more,
And, at the end, he worships virtue and goodness ...

If Man aspires to and inclines towards perfection,
If his soul burst with holy charity,
If he offers himself in sacrifice to his fatherland
If God is God, at last, would it be possible
That he could throw to a common nothingness
vice and virtue ...?

Matter has a law, Life has a law
A supreme law that can never be corrupted ...[68]

El Fiscón Impertinente presented to its readers a poem which had many references to Nuñez's interpretation of Spencerian positivism. The stanzas show the idea that humankind is always improving and, thus, progresses towards a perfect moral world. In particular, the verse that states that there is 'supreme law', a form of providence that governs matter and life and humanity's destiny, depicts the same ideas that Núñez expressed in his article 'La Sociología', which claimed that there are 'superior laws' or sociological factors that are above human laws. Finally, the poem chants that those men who are perfectionist, charitable, loyal to the fatherland demonstrate that 'God is God'. This shows Núñez's backing of religion and his 'subjective belief in the spirit'. The question regarding the possibility of those men throwing themselves to vice and virtue to a 'common nothingness' invokes the idea that it would be impossible for humankind to confuse virtue with vice if God exists. Moreover, it also indicates that there is a wish for a period to come where old values (the ideas of *radicalismo*) are destroyed due to the existence and imposition of the 'supreme law'. The stanzas emphasise the importance of Christian morality in the process of the renovation of humankind.

In 1891, an internal dispute within the National Party in respect to the campaign for the elections of 1892 led to a division among Conservatives

---

[68] Núñez, Rafael. 'Lo invisible', in *el El Fiscón Impertinente, Semanario Literario, Crítico-Burlesco y Joco-Serio*. No. 16. Panamá: 6 de noviembre de 1887, pp. 2–3. p. 18.

who eventually split into two factions: the *Conservadores Nacionales* and the *Conservadores Históricos*. The former were supporters of the Rafael Núñez-Miguel Antonio Caro Formula; the latter, on the other hand, chose General Marceliano Vélez, who was a military leader and hero of the civil war in 1885, as candidate for President. He ran together with his Vice-Presidential candidate Juan Joaquín Ortiz. However, the Conservative and *Liberal Independiente* press focused mainly in comparing Caro and Vélez, on debating who really were defending the true values of conservatism, or defending the *Liberal Independiente*-Conservative alliance. This dispute was a symptom of the first disappointments with the experience of *La Regeneración*, which had not reached the 'horizon of expectations' of *Paz Científica*.

Poetically, *El Constitucional*, contained an article, 'Alea Jacta Est', in 1891. It read as follows:

> The clock of time points, imperturbably, at the appointed hour for a transcendental moment to take place in Colombia. The time will come, and just when it does, those who have participated in the long struggle of the glorious journey of political regeneration will collect its fruits and honours. Those fruits can be collected if there is union between *Liberales Independientes* and Conservatives, those who form the National Party ... [and] if the *Conservadores Históricos*, ... before throwing themselves fearlessly [against *La Regeneración*] ... evoke memories from the past.[69]

The writing showed scepticism when it indicated that 'serious governments should not await for the loyalty of certain people' and forecast that the most probable scenario would be that the government would expel from administrative positions Conservatives that 'were forging castles in the wind'[70] and thinking that they could remain as members of and benefitting from the National Party without being faithful. The author was referring to the *Conservadores Históricos*. Despite the lack of confidence in the good faith of some politicians, *El Constitutional* still looked for ways to solve the dispute between Conservatives, so it supported the candidacy of a third person, Dr José Domingo Ospina Camacho, with the intention of 'partly appeasing over-excited spirits'.[71] This proposal did not prevail, but it was an attempt to unify the ruling *Partido Nacional*.

---

[69] Editorial. 'Alea Jacta Est', *El Constitucional*. Serie 1. N° 2. Panamá: Tipografía de Torres e Hijos, 1 de febrero de 1891, p. 1
[70] Ibid.
[71] Editorial. 'Dr. José Domingo Ospina Camacho', *El Constitucional*. Serie II. N° 12. Panamá: Tipografía de la Torre e Hijos, 19 de abril de 1891, p. 1.

Implicitly, the article denotes a sense that the advance towards progress was still ongoing, but that it could be interrupted if there was division and disloyalty. It indicates that it was time to take a final and risky decision (as Julius Caesar had done when entering Rome). In this sense, there was a requirement to adjust *La Regeneración*'s plan of action, but the expectations seem to remain the same. The solution proposed was either reintegration based on the memory of previous experience of better times when all factions were united, or a political purge of those who abandoned the *Partido Nacional*. Both possible decisions implied the exclusion of *Liberales Radicales*, as well as unfaithful *Conservadores Históricos*, from 'collecting' the benefits of *La Regeneración* when it actually reached its goals.

Ten years later, a newspaper called *El Orden* that claimed to be the printed 'Organ of the Conservative Party of the Isthmus', published 'Corruptio unius est generatio alterius' ('The corruption of one thing is the generation of another'), a text that combined and analysed the political history of Colombia. It began by saying that 'in the physical order as in the moral order lies an inescapable principle: the corruption of one thing is the generation of another'. The text continues by arguing that just as biological matter decays over time, societies also become corrupted because of the effects of 'bad habits'. The article argued that when a society decays, a new one emerges. The article proceeded to apply the same theory to political parties; that they inevitably breakdown due to corruption and deterioration, which are the product of many 'heterogeneous elements' or internal fragmentation that made parties 'impotent' and unable to govern.[72] For *El Orden*, this had happened to the Liberal Party when it divided into different groups in the 1870s. As a consequence, something new was generated: the National Party and *La Regeneración*. In this sense, the article recalled Miguel Antonio Caro's words in his article 'Historia y Filosofía'.

Nonetheless, similar to 'Alea Jacta Est', for the author of 'Corruptio Unius est generatio alterus', the reconstructive era preached by Núñez using the views of Spencer had not yet happened in Panama. He pointed out that the National Party failed because of some corrupt Liberals. In this case, though, it was morally bankrupted *Liberales Independientes* who attracted the support of some members of the Conservative Party.

---

[72] Editorial. 'Corruptio unius est generatio alterus', *El Orden*. Año I. N° 3. Panamá: Imprenta del *Star and Herald*, 17 de septiembre de 1900, p. 1.

Together they formed a 'grotesque alliance, a relaxation of republican practice' and reached power. This text shows disappointment with the results of *La Regeneración*. There was also criticism of the *Conservadores Nacionales* for being untrue to the precepts of conservatism by aligning with the *Liberales Independientes*. The article held that some of the high-ranking members of the Conservative Party, a group of *Conservadores Históricos*, were excluded from government. They opposed and protested against a personalised regime, as a way to preserve, 'like the Church of Christ, truth and morality, [which are the] saving foundations of the Republic'.[73]

Despite the lack of satisfaction with the leadership of *La Regeneración*, the writer also sought for hope in its theories of social renovation. Again, a new course of action was needed, but it had to be led by allegedly true conservatives: the *Conservadores Históricos*. It happened, then, that some of the 'most talented members of the Conservative Party' had managed to gain control of the government, so the article celebrated that '[the] moral sap of the Conservative Party was a saving grace'. The text explained, then, that as a result of the decomposition of the *Partido Nacional*, a new system had emerged and, thus, a transcendental change had occurred in Colombia. In order to make this transformation work, the writer said that it was necessary to return to and maintain the traditional values of conservatism. This would make the institutions more stable. As a result, 'the people, seeing their aspirations fulfilled, will maintain the natural order and justice'.[74]

Here, the constructive stage of history did not begin with *La Regeneración*; it began with the rise of the *Conservadores Históricos*. The article compared them with the Catholic Church, and this link implied that the 'moral sap' of the *Históricos* was imbued in Catholic morality. In other words, the 'saving grace' and the transformation Colombia needed was a renovation based on Catholicism. The salvation of institutions, of the Republic and the happiness of 'the people' depended on it. This messianic and religious rhetoric reflects the conviction that Catholic morality and its conservative defenders had the key to purify society and lead to a better future. Accordingly, since Catholicism and conservatism were at the core of the Colombian population, it was only logical to re-establish traditional values and lifestyles to regenerate the country and obtain 'natural order and justice'. Panamanian *Conservadores Históricos* lost some hope of

[73] Ibid.
[74] Ibid.

the materialisation of peace, social order, tolerance, and progress through the policies of *La Regeneración*, but these ideals did not disappear from their discourse.

After the War of the Thousand Days (1899–1902), the Panamanian press tended towards uncertainty and pessimism. Some of the most significant examples of these were published in *La Probidad*. On 4 October 1903, 'Necesidad de concierto' ('Need for consensus') made a cutting analysis of Núñez's conceptualisation of moral regeneration. The author commented that when Rafael Núñez wrote about political reform, he was not asking for a new legal constitution but instead for a moral reassessment. Furthermore, the editorial argued that, even though the previous Constitution of 1863 did not satisfy the needs of the population, the main reason for its failures was not the document itself but those who were in charge of enforcing it.[75] The article also affirmed that the Constitution of 1886 was better because it ensured protection to all the inhabitants of Colombia and sponsored reciprocal respect for each citizen's rights. Even though the writer deemed the that foundational document as superior to the Constitution of Río Negro, he complained that Colombia was not as advanced as it could be. Its main argument, however, was that moral factors, had made the Constitution of 1886 a failure. Yet the legal document was not to be blamed; instead, 'it is us, with our intransigent [behaviour] and our ambitions and intentions' who are responsible. The author suggested that Colombia look to the past for a solution to its troubles.[76] 'Necesidad de concierto' shows a hint of disappointment regarding *La Regeneración*, criticising the failure of one of its most important foundations: the Constitution of 1886. Nevertheless, the criticism of personal ambition and intransigency and the promotion of reciprocal respect show an encouragement of tolerance, a keystone for achieving *Paz Científica*, by Panamanian conservative intellectuals and column writers.

An editorial of *La Probidad*, 'La Paz', presented a more pessimistic view of the situation in Colombia than 'Necesidad de concierto'. The article was published on 11 October 1903, twenty-three days before Panama became independent from Colombia. It said that after War of the Thousand Days, whilst the 'enemy' had been disarmed, the army reduced in numbers, and the government had been reorganized, the most important issue

---

[75] Editorial. 'Necesidad de concierto', *La Probidad*. Año 1. N° 7. Panamá: Tipografía de G. Crismatt T. 4 de octubre de 1903, p. 1.
[76] Ibid.

was ensuring peace. 'The people' could not rest until the state provided them a guarantee of stability.[77] The author posited that attainment of *Paz Científica* was almost impossible. He said that in Colombia:

> Calm as a product of peace does not exist ... We do not want to be pessimis-tic, but many vows for peace are not sincere ... [and] hatred is still alive and will not be extinguished except ... by means of an elevated order of Christian principles ... [The Government] needs to instill morality into the masses and consolidate its authority.[78]

The article shows that among many *Conservadores Históricos* there was some hope of materialising peace. Moreover, the author explains that even though the War of the Thousand Days ended, the memories of the devas-tation it caused still lingered, causing unease amongst the populace. The writer expressed mistrust, not so much with the ideals of *La Regeneración*, but with the trustworthiness of politicians (especially Liberals) whose adherence to policies that could ensure peacefulness was dubious. In addi-tion, the writer considered that there was still a great deal of resentment between the government, the political elite, and the rest of the population.

Within this context, the author proposed to the governors, Conservatives and the Church, not without a degree of uncertainty and perhaps pessi-mism, to consolidate Christian morality, strong authority and tolerance. That is, as a solution, the writer not only assigned to the government the duty of strengthening the centralised state, but also of requesting the Catholic Church to teach Christian principles. Furthermore, the text encouraged Conservatives to cooperate with the government in its quest to ease 'the task of pacifying, through prudent tolerance, of opposite opin-ions'. If not, said the article, the division among Conservatives 'will lead us to anarchy again'.[79] Once more, it can be noticed that Panamanian Conservatives did not reject the idea that moral renovation and tolerance was necessary to obtain peace and social order, but rather were unsure about the Colombian national government's ability to implement these policies.

---

[77] Editorial. 'La Paz' *La Probidad*. Año 1. N° 8. Panamá: Tipografía de G. Crismatt T., 11 de octubre de 1903, p. 1.
[78] Ibid.
[79] Ibid., p. 2.

PART IV. MORALITY, PROFESSIONALISM AND REGIONALISM IN PANAMANIAN INSTITUTIONS: THE CHURCH, ASSOCIATIONS AND INTELLECTUALS

It was not only the work of political parties in power and their affiliated press to disseminate the discourse of *La Regeneración*. Other institutions, associations and intellectuals informed different interpretations of proper regeneration, morality and development. Examples of these are the Church, the Sociedad 'El Progreso del Istmo', the Sociedad de Medicina y Cirugía de Panamá and prominent intellectuals such as Manuel José Pérez.

The Catholic Church

One of the main representatives of conservative thought in the Isthmus was Bishop José Telésforo Paúl (1831–1889); he was one of the most important voices against liberalism and in favour of a process of purification through the revival of Catholic morality. In Colombia, Paúl was fundamental in the promotion of Conservative thought and in the consolidation *La Regeneración* and of the Church's resurgence in the political, social, cultural and intellectual scene.

According to his own writings, as a Jesuit, he had vowed to live in retreat and silence, before becoming Bishop of Panama in 1875.[80] Paúl remained in this position until 1884, when he became Archbishop of Colombia until his death in 1889. As such, he was an influential force in the design of the Constitution of 1886. This, as mentioned, granted the Executive of the State special laws to govern Panama. Moreover, he was involved in the negotiation of the Concordat between Colombia and the Vatican of 1887, which assigned the Catholic Church the task of managing some public schools in Colombia.[81]

In 1876, he wrote his first Pastoral Letter to the believers of Panama. There, he showed his notion of Catholic patriotism. This had two aspects. The first was strongly reactionary against the Enlightenment origins of

---

[80] José Telésforo Paúl. Bishop of Panama. *Carta Pastoral del Illmo. Sr. Dr. José Telésforo Paúl, Obispo de Panamá, al venerable clero y fieles de su diócesis*. N° 1. (Panamá: Imprenta del *Star and Herald*: Abril de 1876), p. 2.

[81] Bushnell, *The making of modern* Colombia..., p. 144.

liberal ideas and governance. Claiming that 'all over the Universe', people were 'collecting the bitter fruits of the seeds planted by the pseudo-philosophers' of the eighteenth century, Paúl defined Enlightenment ideas as a 'cancer' that affected modern society, dragged Colombia back to 'barbarity and paganism' and transformed 'men into God and passions into their master'. He complained that those ideas 'were brought at a bad time to our virginal beaches'. This was a nationalist image contrasting an alleged Colombian original innocence to pernicious foreign ideas that had corrupted the whole world.[82]

He deemed that the implementation of those ideas represented an attack against the Church.[83] José T. Paúl called upon the followers of the Catholic Church to defend their beliefs and joint in 'glorious combat to conquer the Kingdom of God' from the adversaries of the 'sacred interests of Jesus Christ's religion' and its 'civilizing force'.[84]

> Each soldier must work to deserve joining [Christ's] sacred militia. For this to happen … we must turn the weapons of victory against our own passions. There, inside our heart, we must go to destroy God's enemies. Let us take His divine light there to see the monsters that are our sins, and defeat them, and extirpate them from their root. Let us irrigate with ardent tears the field on which our innocence and virtue have fallen, where there are rotting corpses, so that repentance will resurrect them, and Jesus' blood will soak words asking for mercy pronounced by those who have His authority [i.e., the priests] and restore the beauty and strength of such a defeated city. [Once] we have recovered our innocence, let us fly to the field of Light, Truth, and Love, where our divine Captain Jesus Christ awaits for us … let us fly to conquer Heaven … our fatherland … the immortal crown of those who imitate Jesus.[85]

The fragment is full of military imagery, calling upon Catholics to become 'soldiers' and to take up their duty to fight for their faith. Similarly, it attributes Jesus the rank of Captain. José T. Paúl instructed his parish to defeat the enemies of God. He deemed that a voyage inside the 'heart' against passions and sins was an individual task and a campaign of moral

---

[82] Paúl, *Carta Pastoral del Illmo. Sr. Dr. José Telésforo Paúl, Obispo de Panamá, al venerable clero y fieles de su diócesis.* N° 1…, pp. 2–3.
[83] Ibid., p. 7.
[84] Ibid., p. 9.
[85] Ibid., p. 10.

cleansing the whole of society. Paúl's language indicates that the Colombian people were innately innocent, but had lost their way in earthly world or 'defeated city'. In this case, Colombians and Panamanians in particular needed to cry and suffer to repair the damage. There is a metaphor related to farming: only through pain and redemption could their land be made spiritually fertile again and progress. The metaphor of farming is equated to the kind of patriotic action of soldiers. In short, refertilising the moral ground might require giving away life for the sake of two fatherlands. In Paúl's letter, there is no contradiction in appropriating 'cosmopolitan reason' or the universal mission of the Church for both Catholicism and Colombia. In short, his discourse rejected Enlightenment's ideas and liberalism, but it did not reject cosmopolitanism.

The second aspect of his patriotic Catholicism implied a process of inclusion. In this sense, he wrote that for 'inhabitants of this Isthmus' to truly be 'keepers of the holy laws' of God, they must have motivations that are 'just as well as patriotic'. Paúl stated the Isthmus was the 'bridge of the Universe', a simile that repeatedly appears in Panamanian nationalist discourse. He added that '[everyday] men from all countries cross it, and stop in our capital city, who have to judge the whole Republic [i.e., Estados Unidos de Colombia] based on what they see here'. Therefore, he sustained that 'duty and patriotism' had to compel those who deal with 'temporal affairs' (or leading politicians and citizens) to give Panama City the 'splendour demanded by modern civilisation'.[86] Similarly, the Bishop indicated the need for 'identical and even higher motives' to work for the 'good state of Religion in our fatherland'. He pressed Panamanians to practice their Catholic religion, demonstrate piety, and show respect when they were at the church. In addition, he exhorted them to be 'sober and moderate in your conduct, loyal to our commitments, laborious, peaceful and charitable', because that would make visitors from all South and North America, as well as those from the 'Orient and Occident' to keep a dear memory of the country, even if they saw in Panama City signs of 'ruins and material decadence'.[87] Implicitly, he seemed to envision the arrival of travellers from different nations as a key component for the Isthmus' development. Therefore, his pastoral letter implies keeping a tolerant posture towards different religious beliefs and cultures. This form of patriotism reflected positively on Panama and the rest of the nation, showing the

[86] Ibid., p. 11.
[87] Ibid.

cosmopolitan character of Catholicism as, for him, civilisation depended more on moral behaviour than material wealth.

Paúl was not only critical of Panamanian material conditions, but also of society. He said that Isthmian families maintain a tradition of 'honouring … the founders of this cultured society', and of being humble, united and 'consistently generous' with charitable causes for the 'public wellbeing'. But, even if the practice of religion 'withstands due to the piety of families that give mite to the poor', there was something still missing. Indeed, all those values and traditions were 'a solid base which is necessary to construct the building of social regeneration'. Paúl continued by saying that the 'sum of [all] customs leaves much to be desired'. He challenged those who did not agree with him to 'compare what we are [in the present], with the [future] ideal of [being like] those peoples regenerated by Jesus'.[88] The Bishop listed the vices of Isthmian society: impiety, immoderate desire for enrichment, resentment and hate, licentious behaviour and 'versatile conduct' (or moral flexibility) and 'fear of the unsustained murmur of the fools'. He urged Panamanians to change this for stable behaviour, moderation, strong convictions, the practice of religion, humility, a profound sense of justice and observation for others' rights, and faith and 'Christian chastity'.

Paúl highlighted chastity, because it represented 'the strength and elevation of the spirit, a balm that preserves bodies from eternal death by giving them the germ of celestial Resurrection!' Furthermore, he called upon all the priests to provide their 'indispensable and powerful aid' to transform such an ideal of 'civilising regeneration' into 'a reality in the upcoming future'.[89] The Bishop's pastoral letter precedes Núñez's call for regeneration, but it shares the view that taking society back to a progressive path needed a moral reform. Isthmians possessed an incipient basis to achieve this change, but collaboration with the Church and particularly with the priests was essential to release Panama from material and moral decadence. Regeneration implied two forms of resurrection: a mundane one and a celestial one. For Paúl, a regenerated society that followed Catholic precepts was a mean to reach modernity and also a way to secure the spiritual reward of eternal life.[90]

---

[88] Ibid, p. 12.

[89] Ibid.

[90] To see Paúl's rhetorical evolution and adaptation to different political situations (i.e., the defeat of Conservatives in the Civil War of 1876–1877), and his approximation to Nuñéz's

Associations

Other influential entities in the dissemination not only of knowledge, but of cosmopolitan senses of morality were the cultural and scientific associations linked to the elites and to political power. This was a general tendency in Colombia. In her study about Antioquía and the relation between associations and the promotion of 'morality', Patricia Londoño-Vega indicates that 'cultural associations ... combined improvement of the intellect and morals of their members with promotion of the material development of the community'. She explains that '[a]lthough these organizations had few members, their influence may have been substantial in a small-town milieu'.[91] She analyses a particular association of medical doctors, the *Academia de Medicina de Medellín*, who 'promoted science and education'. The association formed in July 1887 and accompanied a publication called *Anales de la Academia de Medicina de Medellín*. Londoño-Vega indicates that its aims were to 'reinforce professional identity, exchange experiences, increase the flow of up-to-date information, and advise the local government on health and sanitation policies'. More importantly, she explains that the creation of the *Academia de Medicina de Medellín* was approved by the governor. However, she cites how these doctors proposed policies particular to their region. They 'diagnosed the unsanitary conditions of [Medellín] and proposed a number of significant reforms'.[92] From Londoño-Vega's study, it is possible to note the doctors' elitist motivation, but also an interest in influencing regional politics and fomenting scientific education with the support of the authorities. Regarding the influence of professional groups on regional politics and regionalism, it might be useful to add Safford's point about how engineers in Colombia 'did not form a single fraternity'. There were rivalries 'between [different] sectors of the country' and these 'found expression in the development of separate professional communities with distinctive regional styles'.[93] In this section, I will discuss the input of two Panamanian

regeneration, and Rafael Núñez's approximation to see, respectively: José Telésforo Paúl. Obispo de Panamá. *El Obispo de Panamá al Congreso de Colombia. Exposición que hace el Obispo de Panamá al Congreso de los Estados Unidos de Colombia.* (Bogotá: Imprenta Echeverría y Hermanos, 1878); and, José Telésforo Paúl. *Carta Pastoral de José Telésforo Paúl al venerable clero y fieles de su diócesis.* (Panamá: Imprenta del *Star and Herald*, 1883).

[91] Patricia Londoño-Vega. *Religion, Culture, and Society in Colombia. Medellín and Antioquia 1850–1930.* (Oxford: Oxford University Press, 2002), p. 255.

[92] Ibid., pp. 251–252.

[93] Safford, *Ideal of the Practical*, p. 209.

associations: the *Sociedad 'El Progreso del Istmo'* (The Society 'Progress of the Isthmus') and *Sociedad de Medicina y Cirugía de Panamá* (Society of Medicine and Surgery of Panama).

Sociedad 'El Progreso del Istmo'

On 28 November 1889, the *Sociedad 'El Progreso del Istmo'* held a reunion to celebrate Panama's independence from Spain. In a short pamphlet published by Tipografía M. R. de la Torre, the members of this society compiled the proceedings of their *velada literaria* (literary night). The pamphlet does not provide much information about the nature of their regular meetings or the society itself. There are no specific details about regulations or the requirements for affiliation. However, there was a list of members who attended the event. Among the most notable ones there were the first President of this association, Jerónimo de la Ossa (or Gerónimo Ossa); his brother and Mayor of Panama City, José Francisco de la Ossa; Gerardo Ortega, Governor of Panama in 1879; poet Tomás Martín Feulleit; writer Julio Ardila; Rodolfo and Gustavo de Roux, brothers of Luis de Roux, who was a Senator and Representative of the Department of Panama in Bogotá in 1903; and the new Vice-President of the *Sociedad 'El Progreso del Istmo'*, Gaspar Arosemena.[94]

The activities of that evening reflected much regionalist sentiment. Possibly, the most relevant speech was that by Jerónimo de la Ossa. He had studied civil engineering and taught mathematics for several years in Chile. When he returned to Panama, he worked for the *Compagnie Universelle du Canal Inter-Oceanique*. He also wrote poems and hymns, including the lyrics for Panama's future national anthem *Himno Istmeño* (Isthmian Anthem). Just as important, he was the brother-in-law of Manuel Amador Guerrero, the first constitutional President of Panama. After explaining that he was stepping down from the association's presidency, he said:

> This society upholds the duties and rights of the sons of the Isthmus, and is called upon to have a weight in the scales of the destinies of this continental

[94] Other members who I could not identify clearly were Gaspar Pacheco, Emilio Briceño, Conrado Arosemena, Augusto Clement and Carlos Clement, José F. de Alba, Geremías Jaén, Gavino Gutiérrez, J. L. Paniza, José J. de Ycaza, Ramón Luna, Francisco Alvarado, Ezequiel Villamil. *See: Sociedad 'El Progreso del Istmo'. Velada literaria en celebración del 28 de noviembre 'Sociedad El Progreso del istmo'.* (Panamá: Tipografía de M. R. de la Torre e Hijos, 1889), p. 3.

bridge that God ... created to be the future capital of the new civilization and the happy fortune of the awakening world.[95]

De la Ossa's choice of words implies that, eventually, there was going to be a rupture between present and future. Panama was not divinely pre-determined to become the capital of the existing civilization, but of a new and better one. This new civilised world was in an embryo or latent stage and still needed to be fully awakened. It is at that moment in the future that Panama will fulfil its destiny.

De la Ossa added that all 'peoples' (i.e., nations) move forward. As this happens, 'the portentous discoveries of science and art elevate the soul to new heights and unveil the secrets of infinite intelligence'. It is not clear that the awakening of the new world requires a regeneration, but De la Ossa's phrases mean that progress was unavoidable. Yet, for getting onto the wave of constant perfectibility, 'each and every one of us ... within the egoism of family [i.e., Isthmians], the most sacred kind of egoism, desire to rise [to those elevated stages of civilisation] on our own efforts and for our own sake'. He emphasised that, 'first, there is love for those beings that are linked to us ... by bondages of blood, and then, there are the duties imposed on us by our social position'. So, *La Sociedad 'El Progreso del Istmo'* had to work towards transforming the Isthmus into the new capital of civilization for two reason: fraternity among compatriots and their obligations as members of the elites to the rest of the population. Due to this local bonding, 'the members of this society ... Colombians by heart, have a predilection for the Isthmus'.[96] In spite of the adaptation of elements of the 'cosmopolitan reason' when suggesting that progress would be brought by science and the arts, and when picturing Panama as a capital of the world, the *Sociedad 'El Progreso del Istmo'* proposed a project of abjection that somewhat excluded the rest of Colombians.

De la Ossa also pointed out some of the plans of the *Sociedad 'El Progreso del Istmo'* to achieve its modernising goals for the benefit of Panama. He explained that they 'have founded this society to mutually protect ourselves, so that all the sons of the Isthmus, of all colours and parties have a common

---

[95] Geronimo Ossa. 'Discurso'. Velada literaria en celebración del 28 de noviembre 'Sociedad El Progreso del istmo'. (Panamá: Tipografía de M. R. de la Torre e Hijos, 1889), p. 4.

[96] Ibid.

core where they can find resources to raise their spirit in trying times'. The appropriation of 'cosmopolitanism' as an exceptional value of the Isthmians reflects elements that reminds of the discourse of *Paz Científica*, when stating that the *Sociedad 'El Progreso del Istmo'* will embrace Panamanians of all political factions and 'of all colours' (meaning racial and ethnic background) background to provide solace to their spirits. This, at least discursively, carries within a principle of tolerance and a search for consensus in debates about the future of the Isthmus.

Although changing political alignments was common, my limited research shows that the members of the *Sociedad 'El Progreso del Istmo'* had indeed different political orientations. De la Ossa was probably conservative due to his connections with Manuel Amador Guerrero; the De Roux brothers were probably conservatives or *Liberales Independientes*, as their brother Luis de Roux occupied political positions in *La Regeneración*'s government; Gerardo Ortega represented the *Liberales Independientes* when he was Governor of Panama in 1879; Garpar and Conrado Arosemena were likely liberals or moderate liberals, because of their family connections with Justo Arosemena and/or Pablo Arosementa. Tomás Martin Feuillet was probably related to the romantic poet of the same name. José Ardila belonged to a family that had traditionally followed the *Liberales Radicales*. In practice, then, this society did seem to be somewhat politically inclusive. Adding that the *Sociedad 'El Progreso del Istmo'* was there for Panamanians during difficult times suggests implicitly that there was a sense of fear of decadence or perception of crisis, but offering solace to people of all political creeds appears here as a solution for overcoming it.

According to de la Ossa, they wanted to demonstrate that Panamanians could demonstrate respect to Colombia by 'maintaining national integrity', and at the same time show to 'our brothers in Colombia that in our bosom it is possible to find [qualities]... such as intelligence, instruction, valour and patriotism ...' Therefore, the second main purpose of this association was to 'devote all its efforts to enhance the instruction of all Isthmians ... [and] cultivate the intellectual qualities of the youth'.[97] Education was crucial to acquire those goals of progress in the science and arts, joining the waves of that would lead Panama to become the capital of a new civilisation, and also to preserve that condition.

Finally, de la Ossa told his audience that he was ceding his position as President of the *Sociedad 'El Progreso del Istmo'* based on the 'law of alternatibility, which is part of our creed'. This too brings to mind some of

[97] Ibid.

Rafael Núñez's comments regarding how to regenerate the nation: alternating power was necessary to have social and political balance. At the end of the speech, he compelled his successor to preserve the regionalist character of their association and celebrated that 'the flag of our *Sociedad* ... shows this immutable legend: "The Isthmus [is] for the Isthmians".'[98]

On that night, the new President was not present. So, following de la Ossa's speech, the new Vice-President, Gaspar Arosemena, gave an investment speech on his behalf. He expressed admiration for de la Ossa, for his great dedication to 'social affairs' and forecasted that his deeds ensured 'abundant fruits in the coming eras'. This also guaranteed 'good auspices' to the *Sociedad 'El Progreso del Istmo'*. That is, it was prepared to realise its goal. The association, he said, 'cannot do less than realising its patriotic aims'.[99] From all the goals that de la Ossa listed, Gaspar Arosemena highlighted one: 'popular instruction'.[100] He added that:

> The study I have made of the political advancement of the world has convinced me that liberty and instruction are twin sisters that cannot separate from each other without reciprocal damage.[101]

Progress, then, required both instruction on liberty and liberty of instruction. That is, giving the people freedom without proper instruction would cause excess of liberty within a frame of ignorance and, therefore, lack of self-control. Also, providing an excessively prescriptive and restrained education would limit the people's free will and of free thinking. This 'reciprocal damage' was a synonym of social decline. The adequate and balanced combination of instruction and liberty served to establish order and political advancement.

Gaspar Arosemena used as an example Greece and Rome. According to him, both civilisations had once enjoyed liberty, but they had lost it because they developed a kind of 'sense of superiority that distinguished [them]'. This was caused, Gaspar Arosemena said, by the 'lack of moral force that is granted by enlightenment and the knowledge of individual

---

[98] Ibid., p. 5.
[99] Gaspar Arosemena. Untitled Speech. Velada literaria en celebración del 28 de noviembre 'Sociedad El Progreso del istmo'. (Panamá: Tipografía de M. R. de la Torre e Hijos, 1889), p. 6.
[100] Ibid.
[101] Ibid.

rights'.[102] He stated that all the peoples who had become truly free had to abandon first their 'clothing of ignorance'.[103] Paradoxically, it seems that the pride of Greeks and Romans had made them ignorant after they had created a free society. This reminds of a sort of positivist and conservative discourses that portrayed the establishing of civilisations as good, but also that also presented unchecked freedom and uncontrollable progress as a source of disorder. In this case, excessive pride implied the disrespect for individual rights. Enlightenment, that is, the rule of reason and science, was necessary to acquire and preserve a 'moral force'. He added that the objective of the *Sociedad 'El Progreso del Istmo'* was to 'help the Isthmian people to place the foundations of their own liberty, making an effort to raise them to a high cultural level'.[104] For him, it could not be denied that the 'Isthmus possesses very fertile elements' to reach that high level of culture. He continued saying that Panamanian schools were an 'eloquent proof' of the Isthmus' potential for achieving such a goal.

> The recent verified exams reveal the enviable qualities that our youth of both genders have to zealously fulfill the glorious mission that the future keeps for them, and for these triumphs that fortune preserves in an arcane mystery for that intelligent youth we must recognize ... the talent and merit of one man [Simón Araujo].[105]

Gaspar Arosemena did not focus on tangible material or economic progress. His speech gave importance to attaining a high 'cultural level' as a civilizational process. Like Manuel José Pérez, as will be seen later, he seemed to argue that there were other aspects of progress that were more urgent than pure material growth. In this case, it was not a morality based on religious views, but on the more secular civic values that would allow for cultural growth. This involved the acquisition of enlightened ideas, especially the cosmopolitan notion of individual rights. For him, the Isthmus was ready to engage in this journey for the Panamanian youth had been tested and they had shown the monitors (i.e., adults and teachers) that they were on the right track towards bringing modernity to the Isthmus. That is, their agency seemed to be tamed, and fears of misguidance and misconduct had been reduced. Gaspar Arosemena seemed to

[102] Ibid.
[103] Ibid.
[104] Ibid.
[105] Ibid.

combine hope and assurance of a better future. His words manifested confidence in Panamanian youth's potential, but he presented their aims as projected into the future. There is progress, but the main goal had not been achieved yet.

Gaspar Arosemena exalted the figure of Simón Araujo as the main architect to such a state of advancement in education. It has been difficult to find information about Araujo's life. He was a Colombian Liberal politician. He began studies in different disciplines in various countries, but he never finished.[106] Araujo arrived in Panama possibly in the early 1880s. He founded and directed a private school: El Colegio del Istmo.[107] It is known that he provided furniture and some teaching material to the Colegio Balboa.[108] Gaspar Arosemena lamented that Araujo had to leave Panama. On behalf of the *Sociedad 'El Progreso del Istmo'*, he expressed that 'knowing of his absence produced great sorrow on the heart of Isthmian patriots'.[109] The fact that a group of people that denominated themselves as Isthmian patriots granted so much credit to a Colombian is curious. Nonetheless, this same deed reveals three interesting features of the *Sociedad 'El Progreso del Itsmo'*: first, the group was patriotic or proto-nationalist, but Colombian nationality still remained as part of its members' identity to the point that they welcomed other Colombians into the inner core of the social elite. Second, it shows that there were direct connections between the members of this cultural association and leading educators. These links were essential for the rise of the pedagogical elite. Third, these specially selected members of the educational community were worthy of admiration and social embracement, regardless of their place of birth, for their work in setting up the basis for modernisation. The fact that, in Gaspar Arosemena's viewpoint, Araujo helped to establish a promising stage of culture in Panama not only made him a 'tamer of

---

[106] Instituto Educativo Simón Araujo. '¿Quién fue Simón Araujo?' in https://iesimonaraujo.edu.co/simon-araujo/

[107] José Agustín Torres. Informe del Inspector General de Instrucción Pública de Panamá, in *Informe Presentado al Congreso de Colombia en su Sesión de 1888.* (Bogotá: unclear publisher, 1888), p. 148.

[108] Abel Bravo. *Informe del Colegio Balboa.* República de Colombia – Departamento de Panamá – Colegio Balboa – Rectoría – Numero 8 – Panamá, Abril 24 de 1890, *Informe que el Ministro de Instrucción Pública presenta al Congreso de Colombia en sus sesiones de 1890.* (Bogotá: Imprenta de 'La Luz', 1890), p. 294.

[109] Gaspar Arosemena. 'Untitled Speech' in *Sociedad 'El Progreso del Istmo'.* Velada Literaria … p. 6.

agency', but also what I call a "domesticator of youth", as his actions put students at the service of their homeland.

At the end of his speech, Gaspar Arosemena reinstated the idea that the *Sociedad 'El Progreso del Istmo'* had an 'egoistic character'. He clarified that it was not a self-centred attitude that provoked envy for the happiness of others, nor that it promoted the enjoyment of others' disgrace. Instead, its egoism is 'encrypted in the desire for the general good'. This 'Holy egoism', as he described it, was the same as 'patriotism', which 'in front of the fatherland absorbs it all'.[110] He complained that the members of the association were accused of having 'low intentions', or of betraying Colombia. Yet he ensured that this was not the case. 'For more than half a century we have participated in the sorrows and joys of Colombia.' For him it was wrong to accuse Panamanians of having 'a heart lacking of all noble sentiments' and to think that they wanted to 'cut with one strike a vinculum that emerges from the bottom of the soul'.[111] Nevertheless, Gaspar Arosemena argued that this loyalty did not impede the members of *Sociedad 'El Progreso del Istmo'* to have a 'predilection for the Isthmus'. He sustained that working for one section of Colombia was useful for its whole. Hence 'by lifting the moral level of the Isthmus, we give impulse to the progress of Colombia'. Finally, to support de la Ossa's speech, he claimed that saying 'the Isthmus for the Isthmians' was not a manifestation of 'petty passions'; it was an 'echo of the general opinion' in Panama. This opinion did not advocate for independence, instead it 'aspired at only breaking the chain that ties [us], like another Prometheus, to the dire rock of immobility'.[112]

From this, it can be inferred that the 'popular instruction' that the *Sociedad 'El Progreso del Istmo'* sought to provide did not have the goal of instilling feelings against the rest of Colombia. Nonetheless, it did aim at educating a youth that worked mainly in favour of the Isthmus. Allegedly, this was, as Gaspar Arosemena suggested, a general demand. In order to achieve the 'high level of culture' mentioned at the beginning of his speech, the most important goal of educators and the educated youth was to elevate the 'moral level' of Panama. By adding that belonging to Colombia resulted in 'immobility', Gaspar Arosemena insinuated that the poor situation of values in Panama caused both moral and material

[110] Ibid., pp. 6–7.
[111] Ibid., p. 7.
[112] Ibid., p. 7.

stagnation. Thus, the most relevant role of Isthmian instruction was to change the moral inertia, and produce moral progress to lift Panama up to a higher state of civilisation. As a collateral effect, the moral and cultural situation of Colombia would also improve. Hence, the patriotic 'predilection for the Isthmus' was inherently a form of Colombian nationalism.

Sociedad de Medicina y Cirugía de Panamá

In a similar fashion, on 28 November 1898, a group of Panamanian and foreign physicians both from Panama and abroad[113] gathered to found the *Sociedad de Medicina y Cirugía de Panamá*.[114] The doctors also agreed to publish a bulletin, the content of which was primarily news regarding local medical problems, translations of foreign medical articles and treatments for different diseases.[115]

The *Boletín de la Sociedad de Medicina y Cirugía de Panamá* (*Bulletin of the Society of Medicine and Surgery of Panama*) detailed the nature, objectives and leadership of the society. A statute published in the *Boletín* described the group as a 'scientific corporation' with the specific purpose of creating a strong network of doctors in the Isthmus; study and solve issues in its field of expertise; work for the advancement of medicine in Colombia; raise the prestige of the medical career; and fight 'empiricism' and 'charlatanism'.[116] In addition, the periodical republished articles about new surgical methods; and remedies for diseases such as tuberculosis or problems with sight. These were published mainly in France, but also in the United States, Germany and Great Britain. Some of this information was received through Panamanian or Colombian doctors that were studying or visiting those countries.[117] Furthermore, this periodical reported about daily health problems affecting the Isthmus (including statistics

---

[113] José E. Calvo and Julio Icaza. 'Prospecto', *Boletín de la Sociedad de Medicina y Cirugía de Panamá*. Vol. 1, no. 1, Panamá: Sociedad de Medicina y Cirugía de Panamá, 15 de enero de 1899, p. 1.

[114] Ibid.

[115] This can be observed by looking at all scientific articles published between 15 January 1899 and 15 August 1899.

[116] 'Estatutos de la Sociedad de Medicina y Cirugía de Panamá', *Boletín de la Sociedad de Medicina y Cirugía de Panamá*. Año. 1, No. 1, Panamá, 15 de Enero de 1899, p. 14.

[117] See: de Pablo de Obarrio. 'Contribución al estudio de la catarata congénica', *Boletín de la Sociedad de Medicina y Cirugía de Panamá*. Año 1, No. 5, Panamá, 15 de mayo de 1899, pp. 75–77. Pablo de Obarrio was studying at in the Laboratory of Histology of the Institute of Physiology of the University of Berlin under the supervision of a Dr Fritch.

about deaths and ill persons). One of the main concerns of the *Sociedad de Medicina y Cirugía*, though, was to enhance the professionalisation of the medical career and to instruct the population about the benefits of consulting graduates with proper scientific knowledge about medicine.

The editors, Dr José E. Calvo and Dr Julio Icaza, explained in the 'Prospecto' (Prospectus) of the *Boletín* that the foundation of the *Sociedad de Medicina y Cirugía* was a 'patriotic project'. To show this, the date of its foundation was 28 November, 'anniversary of the glorious independence of the Isthmus from Spain.[118] Other members of the *Sociedad de Medicina y Cirugía* celebrated the place of the meeting, the premises of the Municipal Council, because 'it retains for the Isthmian people, perennial patriotic remembrances'.[119] Even though the *Sociedad de Medicina y Cirugía* had a regionalist nature, the *Boletín* established that it would reject any 'insult' against the 'honour and dignity' of the Republic of Colombia, 'for we proudly take shelter under its beautiful pavilion'.[120] In regard to its area of expertise and for procuring the development of medicine, the 'Prospecto' of the *Boletín* said that the *Sociedad de Medicina y Cirugía*, as a patriotic entity, would be dedicated to studying the problems of public hygiene, for 'the Isthmus' future fortune' depended on their solution.[121] The language used in the *Boletín* showed a connection with the ideal of *La Regeneración*: the *Sociedad de Medicina y Cirugía* would be dedicated to the 'moral progress' of Panama[122] and would remain impartial; not engaging in disputes between the national political parties.[123]

In addition, Calvo and Icaza opposed 'empiricism' and 'charlatanism'. They stated that the *Sociedad de Medicina y Cirugía* would not allow polemic debates with 'charlatans' who tried to exploit the 'ignorance of the masses'. These two doctors argued that the purpose of their Society was to eradicate that 'plague' from Panama City. They complained that, at the time, doctors did not have any other defence from 'empirics [and] charlatans' than the good judgement of other professionals.[124] Perhaps, though, Dr Santos José Aguilera (1860–1924) was more explicit and

---

[118] Calvo and Icaza, 'Prospecto', p. 1.
[119] Santos José Aguilera, 'Speech with no title', in Ibid., p. 3.
[120] Calvo and Icaza. 'Prospecto', in Ibid., p. 2.
[121] Ibid.
[122] Ibid.
[123] Ibid.
[124] Ibid.

concise when describing the aims of the *Sociedad de Medicina y Cirugía*. He wrote in the following manner:

> Fortune has provided a solemn day for a transcendental event ... to organize and constitute a medical and surgical society that gives to our profession stature, moral and intellectual representation – and so ... the society [i.e., Panamanians] we serve would not overpower our rights. In association we will be less exposed to the insults of people without [scientific] authority from newspapers [that want] to satisfy their alleged holy will or to write something sensational.[125]

His words imply an elitist sense of professionalism linked to patriotism ('the solemn day', mentioned above, being 28 November 1899). Although it is not clear who the 'people without authority' were, it is likely that Santos Aguilera referred to individuals who tried vehemently to discredit doctors; newspapers that published false information, such as adverts for inefficient medicines; those who argued that they could practise medicine based on knowledge acquired through experience; and persons who opposed doctors for political, commercial, or personal reasons.[126]

The creation of the *Sociedad de Medicina y Cirugía* had an ulterior *raison d'être*. Drawing from Santos José Aguilera, it can be inferred that it was not an entity dedicated exclusively to scientific progress, but also focused on defending the rights and enhancing the social and political influence of doctors. The notion that doctors and surgeons needed 'moral representation' denotes a sense of alterity: doctors are opposed to the "others" or unreasonable persons who comment about medicine and science without having proper comprehension. These are portrayed as immoral. In contrast, studying for and possessing a degree creates a hierarchy of knowledge and grants to a few the authority to reason about and practice medicine. In order to secure this moral and scientific authority, the members of the *Sociedad de Medicina y Cirugía* needed a network and support from other professionals and government representatives, who were seen as equal or at least allies in social standards. In other words, this professional association represented a group of people who saw themselves as part of the scientific elite which, besides its altruistic endeavours, also attempted to obtain social and political influence.

---

[125] Santos José Aguilera, 'Speech with no title', in Ibid., p. 3.
[126] No author. 'Médicos por intuición', *Boletín de la Sociedad de Medicina y Cirugía de Panamá*, Ano I. N. 3 Panamá: Marzo 15 de 1899, pp. 47–48.

Indeed, some members of the *Sociedad de Medicina y Cirugía* occupied high political positions before and after 1903. For instance, Santos
José Aguilera worked in jails, asylums, the police and fire departments,
and several public hospitals, such as the Hospital Santo Tomás.
According to one biography, he was known as 'doctor of the poor'.[127]
Later on, the *Sociedad de Medicina y Cirugía de Panamá* would accept
a membership request from Dr Luis de Roux,[128] whose brothers, as
mentioned, were members of the *Sociedad 'El Progreso del Istmo'*, while
he became one of the last representatives of the Department of Panama
to the Government of Colombia. Nonetheless, the most significant
founding member was the first president of the association, Dr Manuel
Amador Guerrero.[129]

The *Boletín* also presented critical views of the other aspects of society, such as the disregard for formal education. In an article with the
title 'Médicos por Intuición' ('Doctors by Intuition'), *El Boletín de la
Sociedad de Medicina y Cirugía de Panamá* complained about the lack
of regulation in the awarding of degrees in medicine. For them, setting
controls to the practice of medicine was of utmost importance because
'our people are too credulous and prone to [believe in any] marvelous
thing'. They claimed that charlatans knew this, and 'take advantage to
transform the crowd into fanatics, concealing, with fake generosity, a
sinister *arriere pensée* [or ulterior goal] that most of the time is undeni-
ably directed against society in general, and, in particular, against [the
doctor's] guild'.

The author of the article argued that, due to the weak guidelines concerning medical certifications, many 'self-graduated' doctors practised ille-
gally around the country. However, the article not only deemed that it was
necessary to establish a regulatory body for the sake of protecting professional doctors, but also because it was reflected badly on educational bodies and education in Panama and Colombia in general. The article
protested against the fact that anyone could practise a profession without
having the proper experience and that this negatively affected those who
'had taken their profession seriously and had done conscientious study to

---

[127] *Biografías Panameñas.* Biblioteca Nacional de Panamá. www.binal.ac.pa
[128] 'Misceláneas. Nuevo Colega', *Boletín de la Sociedad de Medicina y Cirugía de Panamá.*
Año. 1, No. 8, Panamá, 15 Agosto de 1899, pp. 149.
[129] Ibid., pp. 2–3.

exercise it ... for the love of science, in the midst of limitations and sacrifices that are not always properly recognised and well paid'. This undermined the importance of the 'heroic and sustained struggle of searching for a professional degree' and discouraged the pursuit of education.[130]

In order to illustrate the point better, the article presented an analogy about a character called Perdomo, a 'famous charlatan' who went to Bogotá 'pretending to be the successor of Christ and apostle of charity'. This personage ridiculed those doctors who charged for their work by pretending that he was not interested in remuneration. There was a group of people who spread 'propaganda' for him, but later they had to repent. For the editors of *El Boletín de la Sociedad de Medicina y Cirugía de Panamá*, this was a moralising story about adequate social behaviour. Besides the care of individual health, there were other matters that doctors should safeguard and act upon:

> The respect for the sanctuary of the household, to which no entry should be allowed to anyone except for those persons of unquestionable moral probity, to impede the profanation of a profession deemed as true priesthood in every civilised nation.[131]

The demand for formal professional education intended to attain sponsorship for the creation of a scientific elite that would define how the policy-makers and the rest of the population should construe and uphold science and rationality for the advancement of Panama and Colombia, enabling them to join other 'civilised nations'. That is, their discourse was, in principle, connected to cosmopolitan values. Nevertheless, the members of the *Sociedad de Medicina y Cirugía* showed contempt for the 'ignorance of the masses', putting down the intellectual qualities of the majority, and for those who supposedly learned medicine empirically. Using the story of Perdomo as an allegory through incorporating a religious language, they rejected false prophets and portrayed themselves as preachers of scientific knowledge. In doing so, they also connected the *Sociedad de Medicina y Cirugía* and doctors to the discourse of *La Regeneración*: science, morality and order were key for regeneration and progress. Therefore, part of the doctors' work was messianic. These doctors attributed to themselves a mission of educating and implanting 'moral

---

[130] Ibid., p. 48. In the same issue of the bulletin, a follow-up article called 'Sobre Farmacia' (On Pharmacy) consistently argued the same for the profession of pharmacist. Ibid., pp. 48–49.

[131] Ibid., p. 48.

probity' into the rest of the population. This had to be done through the spread of Science and the elimination of unreasonability and belief in the 'marvellous'. The salvation of society, though, also depended on the eradication of complete freedom to practice medicine that resulted in a lack of order and damaged individual and public health. It was immoral and meant stagnation. The solution was a rationalised verification of proper training to honour and decontaminate the provision of health services.

Through the *Junta de Higiene* (Hygiene Council), Isthmian doctors attempted to establish a body that institutionalised and controlled the practice of medicine. At a session of the *Sociedad de Medicina y Cirugía* held on 1 March 1899, Dr Julio Icaza and Dr Indalecio Camacho to requested the Prefect of the Province of Panama to impose regulations with the purpose of controlling the exercise of medicine in the capital. These rules demanded that every person who practised medicine in Panama must hand over their diplomas to the *Junta de Higiene*. If they could not or if they did not get a 'pass' and approval of the *Junta*, then, the applicant should be 'categorically prohibited to continue practising medicine' in Panama City. After a debate, in which Manuel Amador Guerrero and other members opposed the proposal, the majority of the members approved the motion.[132] There is no information about what happened next or to what extent this measure was accepted, promulgated and implemented by governmental authorities. It is likely, though, this process was suspended due to the beginning of the War of the Thousand Days.

Since the *Sociedad de Medicina y Cirugía de Panamá* aimed at professionalising medical careers and securing adequate training to form a scientific elite, it could not operate independently from the formation and consolidation of a pedagogical elite. The fact that Nicolás Victoria Jaén and Mélchor Lasso de la Vega, and occupied the office of Secretary of Public Instruction and Justice during Manuel Amador Guerrero's presidency (1904–1908), hints at a connection between the views of the *Sociedad de Medicina y Cirugía* and those of.[133]

---

[132] *Sociedad de Medicina y de Cirugía de Panamá.* 'Sección Oficial. Acta de la Sesión de la Sociedad del 1 de marzo de 1899 – Presidencia del Doctor Manuel Amador Guerrero', *el Boletín de la Sociedad de Medicina y Cirugía de Panamá*. Año 1. No. 4, Panamá: 15 de abril de 1899, p. 1.
[133] Ibid., p. 3.

Panamanian Conservative Philosophy during La Regeneración: *Manuel José Pérez*

Manuel José Pérez was possibly the best-known conservative intellectual of the period. Many of his texts were compiled and published in 1888 by the press of M. R. de la Torre e Hijos in *Ensayos Morales, Políticos y Literarios* (Moral, Political and Literary Essays). After acknowledging his friendship with Manuel José Pérez in the 'Prólogo', Pablo Arosemena expressed pride in his Panamanian peers; liberal intellectuals such as Justo Arosemena and Gil Colunje; politician José de Obaldía; and poet Tomás Martín Feuillet. It then pointed out the underlying principles of Perez's essays: there must be a search for balanced progress that combines both material and moral improvement.[134]

The book then proceeded to transcribe Pérez's articles. *Ensayos Morales, Políticos y Literarios* includes an article divided in two parts, 'Fenómenos Morales' (Moral Phenomena). The first part began with an intriguing phrase:

> There are things that would be incredible if one were not obligated to surrender to evidence; [these are] moral phenomena that cannot be explained satisfactorily unless one admits that the main constitutive element of [contemporary] societies is the utilitarian theories of Bentham.[135]

He wondered 'if the basis of civilization … is utility only by itself, without any contemplation for equity and justice, where is the so-praised moral progress of the peoples?'[136] Pérez's views did not completely disagree with utilitarian principles. What he argued was that to determine the usefulness of any action, it was compulsory to consider moral aspects for the improvement of society.

He questioned whether the development of the 'self' was the most elevated manifestation of 'humanity's perfectibility', or if instead individual growth implied that 'humankind degenerates as its intelligence advances towards an unknown future'. For him, new discoveries revealed the 'precious secrets of Nature' and gave explanations for what were

---

[134] Pablo Arosemena. 'Prólogo', Manuel José Pérez. *Ensayos Morales, Políticos y Literarios.* (Panamá: Imprenta de M. R. de la Torre, 1888), pp. xx–xxi.

[135] Manuel José Pérez. 'Fenómenos Morales. Primera Parte', *Ensayos Morales, Políticos y Literarios.* (Panamá: Imprenta de M. R. de la Torre, 1888), p. 17.

[136] Ibid.

known as 'mysteries' in preceding centuries. But he rhetorically asked: 'Does moral progress [develop] in an inverse rate to material progress?'[137] The answer was that progress in science and technology of the era was disproportionate and even contrary to the moral progress of humanity. He deliberated about whether it was beneficial to eliminate the metaphysical character of formerly impenetrable phenomena.

'There is a fight between the heart and the head. Thought wants to subordinate everything',[138] he stated. Using a series of poetic metaphors, Pérez counterposed mathematics and science to the metaphysical and the spiritual. In other words, he saw a competition between rationalism and empiricism, on one side, and the spirit, on the other.[139]

On one part, there are numbers, which are rigid and indifferent like cadavers, implacable like eternal justice, or even more than her for they are incapable of mercy; on the other part, there are Faith, Hope, Charity, Love and Goodness ... everything that can be touch, weighed and priceable, on the one side; on the other ... the soul with all its sweetness, and the aspirations to reach infinity with all its promises.[140]

In Pérez's comments, numbers and their link to materialism are not necessarily pernicious. On the contrary, they are just. Yet they are inflexible and do not allow for nuance and compassion. Therefore, they limit the immanent qualities of the spirit: the capacity of having faith and expectations, of being willing to help others, of loving, and of general well-doing. Using the words of Nicola Miller, it is possible to claim that Perez's text presupposes that the aims of achieving technocratic modernity block the arrival to moral modernity. His writings present two different kinds of horizons of expectations: one is based on notions of technocratic modernity or the appreciation of empirical knowledge and methods of giving value to material advancement. The other is a horizon of moral and spiritual expectations. In this sense, 'the aspirations to reach infinity' do not represent, in Perez's text, only a Catholic vision of a better afterlife; it also symbolises perpetual spiritual progress in the earthly world.

Next, he insisted that scientific and technological progress was inevitable but unpredictable, so it signified a potential danger to humanity. This

137 Ibid.
138 Ibid.
139 Ibid.
140 Ibid.

'growing [materialist] progression ... breaks the remaining laces of union that exist between humankind, [creating a] crazed society ... [so] it is possible that we will return to the time of barbarity'.[141] Here, whichever were the earthly advances of humanity, the breaking of bonds meant a moral regression which would eventually lead also to material decadence or a return to worse times in the past. But, as seen in the writings of Caro and in Panamanian conservative newspapers, Perez viewed regression not only as a step forward to obtain spiritual salvation, but also to generate a better earthly future. He talked about the need of catharsis for humans to regenerate. 'Passing through a series of horrors, reliving the terrible scenarios of those mournful times [of the past], a purified and redeemed humanity will return to life through expiation and sacrifice.'[142] This could not happen in any other way, for the morality of all 'peoples' was complete disturbed.[143] Humanity had to surpass the deterioration of universal values to reach perfection in the mundane world and to achieve salvation in the spiritual world.

Maybe this dual vision of regeneration is clearer in 'Fenómenos Morales. Segunda Parte'. There, Pérez apologised because a 'friend' mentioned to him that readers of his previous article could think he had 'retrograde ideas'.[144] This was the result of a 'retreat from [social] life in which you [i.e., Pérez] gladly live', according to this anonymous friend. Pérez did not want his readers to misunderstand his message, so he defended his self-segregation by saying that doing so 'placed him away from the battlefields that are ... the greatly populated [urban] centres'. Adding that, for him, it was like being in the theatre. He was indicating that from his isolation, he could see events objectively from a distance. Pérez indicated that 'since life is ... a continuous comedy, humanity can be seen just as it presents itself, and it is not the fault of the spectator if [human] deeds, far from thrilling him to the point of provoking a strident applause, fill him with sadness to the point of snatching lamentations'.[145] Unlike Job and Jeremias, he continued, these cries were not 'maledictions', but 'the most fervent wish for moral improvement of the peoples mixed with the fear that the easy pleasures of material progress make [moral improvement]

---

[141] Ibid., p. 18.
[142] Ibid.
[143] Ibid.
[144] Manuel José Pérez. 'Fenómenos Morales. Segunda Parte', *Ensayos* ..., p. 20.
[145] Ibid.

fade more and more'.[146] Perez's dilemma was that material progress could give way to libertinage.

He posited that there is a 'perfect equilibrium' in all existing beings and things, however. In the physical world, he asserted, lack of balance caused natural disasters; but, in the moral world, it produced the 'perversion of ideas and the exaltation of feelings … and the decomposition of [good] taste for beauty and truth'. Therefore, he asked, 'if man is composed of spirit and matter …, how would the cult rendered [only] to matter not seem strange …?' The cult to matter was loaded with a conception of progress that 'almost completely ignored' all the factors what could help the perfecting of 'that mysterious fluid that we call soul …'[147] Pérez critiqued that the postulates of 'materialist philosophers such as Karl Vogt, Jacob Moleschott, and Émile Littré were approved by most of learned society.' He also complained that those ideas 'recognised as an incontestable fact that thought is a "product of the brain", just as bile is [a product] of the liver, and urine is [a product] of the kidneys'. For Pérez, society was yielding to materialism, which neglected the abstract character of thought as the fruit of the human mind. However, he still defended that it was necessary to cultivate the 'generative potency [of the mind] without which inert matter would lay in perpetual stagnation or would inevitable decompose'.[148] Pérez, in sum, posited that materialist philosophers had established an atheistic religion of matter. Similar to his comments on Bentham, he did not completely disagree with their ideas and scientific analysis. He did agree with the medical studies that indicated that bile and urine were products of the liver and kidneys. The graphic comparison between these somewhat disgusting and lifeless fluids vis-à-vis thoughts served him to illustrate a notion he perceived as erroneous: the existence of inert thought. For him, thinking had a spiritual element connected to the soul. Therefore, it was mandatory to nurture the spirit in order to prevent thoughts decaying as bile, urine and unanimated matter in general do.

Pérez affirmed that it was possible to achieve both moral and material progress at the same time. He contested that:

---

[146] Ibid.
[147] Ibid., p. 21.
[148] Ibid.

Looking, as much as possible, for an equilibrium between what is moral and what is material, is not and cannot be proof that [someone] embraces ideas against progress. On the contrary, it not only implies having the desire to conserve what already exists, but also to always advance towards that unknown and incomprehensible aim to which humanity presses forward due to its superior disposition.[149]

So, he advised that progress should not always mean total change and a break with the past and the present. Things that already existed were worth preserving, such as traditional moral and religious values. It was, for him, the most reasonable way to secure the expiation of humanity and continue progressing towards modernity.

Conclusion: Legacies of La Regeneración in Panamanian State-Building

At the end of the nineteenth century and early twentieth centuries, as political reform failed and the Isthmus did not progress as its leaders had expected, Panamanian Conservatives, *Liberales Independientes*, and even some *Liberales Radicales* began to link the aims of *La Regeneración* only to Isthmian interests. The main conceptual legacy of *La Regeneración* in terms of constructing Panamanian identity was the notion of *Paz Científica*, because the idea that a calculated peace would bring order and progress became the core of Panamanian nationalist discourse of post-independent Panama.

So, even though Colombian governance was not successful in enacting *La Regeneración*, its discourse imbued with positivism and conservatism did not dissipate in the Isthmus after independence. Panamanian intellectuals leaned towards this rhetoric and practice as evidenced, for example, in Pablo Arosemena's 'Declaración del 4 de noviembre de 1903'. There is more evidence though: for instance, an earlier version of the coat of arms of Panama. It was designed and painted by Conservative lawyer and teacher, Nicanor Villalaz (1855–1932). The original motto of Panama was not '*Pro Mundi Beneficio*' (For the Benefit of the World), but '*Paz, Libertad, Unión y Progreso*' (Peace, Freedom, Union and Progress'), which reiterates the positivist principles of *Paz Científica*. Instead of a winged wheel, it showed a train and telegraph; two symbols of progress in

---

[149] Ibid., p. 21.

Fig. 2.1   An earlier version of the Panamanian Coat of Arms. (1 June 1904). Courtesy of the Museo del Canal Interoceánico de Panamá (MUCI)

positivist discourse. Similarly, in the original version, besides the hanging rifle and a sabre, there was also a dismantled cannon. In both cases, this could be interpreted as a metaphor for peace. The fact that the motto was changed to '*Pro Mundi Beneficio*' later signified a preference for sending out an internationalist message and also, perhaps, an attempt to differentiate Panama from Colombia and its national motto 'Freedom and Order'. All this shows that since the late nineteenth century, both conservatism and conservatised-liberalism informed the ways Isthmian intellectuals and politicians conceived the identities that Panamanian citizens had to develop to achieve a vision of the future that promised moral and material progress. Their ideas continued influencing Panamanian identity-building even after 1903.

BIBLIOGRAPHY

Aparicio, Fernando. 'Represión y explotación en Panamá durante La Regeneración: 1886–1903', *Historia General de Panamá. El Siglo XIX*. Cap. XIII. Tomo III. Vol. II., Castillero Calvo, Alfredo, ed. (Panamá: Comité Nacional del Centenario, 2004), pp. 236–255.

Arce, Enrique and Juan B. Sosa. *Compendio de Historia de Panamá: Texto adoptado oficialmente para la enseñanza en las escuelas y colegios de la nación* (Panamá: Casa Editorial del "Diario de Panamá", 1911).

Arosemena, Pablo. *Escritos*. Tomos I–II. (Panamá: Imprenta Nacional, 1930).

Bayón, Jesús Ferro. 'Núñez y la filosofía política. Apuntes para una historia de las ideas en la Costa', Gustavo Bell Lemus, comp. *El Caribe Colombiano. Selección de textos históricos*. (Barranquilla: Ediciones Uninorte, 1988).

Bravo, Abel. *Informe del Colegio Balboa*. República de Colombia – Departamento de Panamá – Colegio Balboa – Rectoría – Numero 8 – Panamá, Abril 24 de 1890, *Informe que el Ministro de Instrucción Pública presenta al Congreso de Colombia en sus sesiones de 1890*. (Bogotá: Imprenta de 'La Luz', 1890).

Boletín de la Sociedad de Medicina y Cirugía de Panamá. Vol. 1, N° 1 - N° 8 (Panamá: Sociedad de Medicina y Cirugía de Panamá, 15 January 1899–15 August 1899).

Caro, Miguel Antonio. *Escritos Políticos*. Carlos Valderrama Andrade, comp. (Bogotá: Fundación Caro y Cuervo, 1990).

Caro, Miguel Antonio y Rafael Núñez. *Epistolario de Rafael Núñez con Miguel Antonio Caro*. (Bogotá: Instituto Caro y Cuervo, 1977).

Deas, Malcolm. *Del Poder y la Gramática y otros ensayos sobre historia, política y literatura colombianas*. (Bogotá: Tercer Mundo Editores, 1993).

El Aliento. Político, Noticioso y de Variedades. Serie I, N° 1–2 (Panamá: 15 January 1891–30 January 1891).

El Aspirante. Periódico de intereses generales. Año I–IV. N° 1–2, 4–26, 31–32, 37–42, 46, 50, 52, 54, 58–60, 62–65, 67–68, 70, 72–76, 78, 80–82, 84–86, 88–101, 104, 106–108, 111, 114–115, 117–118, 120, 125–126, 130, 139, 142, 147–148, 151, 159, 164 (Panamá: 3 January 1891–15 February 1894).
El Boletín Diocesano., Año I, Año IV. N° 10–11, 19–20, 89–92, 94, 96–109 (Panamá: Diócesis de Panamá, Administración de la Secretaría del Obispado, 15 November 1893–15 December 1897).
El Boletín Electoral de Panamá. Número VIII–X, XII (Panamá: 31 August 1891–5 November 1891).
El Constitucional. N° 1–6, 10–12 (Panamá: 28 January 1891–19 April 1891).
El Derecho. Órgano oficial del Directorio Liberal Independiente del Estado. Año I, N° 2, (Panamá: 25 January 1881).
El Fiscón Impertinente, Semanario Literario, Crítico-Burlesco y Joco-Serio. N° 15–18, 20–21 (Panamá: Imprenta de M. R. de la Torre e hijos, 30 October 1887–18 December 1887).
El Istmeño. Año II. Serie IV. Número 19. (Panamá: 24 May 1884).
El Orden: Órgano del Partido Conservador del Istmo. Año I, N° 1–6, 8–22 (Panamá: Imprenta Star and Herald, 5 September 1900–26 January 1901).
El Precursor: periódico político, industrial, noticioso, comercial i literario. Año I–III, N° 1–4, 7–8, 10–15, 17–58, 60–63, 66, 68, 70, 130 (Panamá: Imprenta de M. R. de la Torre e Hijos, 24 February 1878–25 October 1880).
Instituto Educativo Simón Araujo. '¿Quién fue Simón Araujo?' in https://iesimonaraujo.edu.co/simon-araujo
Koselleck, Reinhart. *The Practice of Conceptual History. Timing History, Spacing Concepts.* Todd Samuel Presner et al., trans. (Stanford: Stanford University Press, 2002).
La Probidad: política, intereses del Istmo y variedades. Año I, N° 5–11 (Panamá: Tipografía de G. Crismatt, 20 September 1903–1 November 1903).
Ministerio Ejecutivo de los Estados Unidos de Colombia. *Constitución política de los Estados Unidos de Colombia de 1863.* (Colombia; 8 May 1863) Accessed: http://www.cervantesvirtual.com/obra-visor/colombia-29/html/02613e70-82b2-11df-acc7-002185ce6064_1.html#I_23_
Molina, Gerardo. *Las Ideas Liberales en Colombia – 1849-1914.* 4ta. Edición. (Bogotá: Ediciones Tercer Mundo, 1974).
Núñez, Rafael, *La Reforma Política* en Colombia. Tomos I–Tomo VI. (Bogotá: Editorial A B C – Biblioteca Popular de Cultura Colombiana, 1945).
Núñez, Rafael. *La Reforma Política en Colombia.* (Bogotá: no information, 1888).
Núñez, Rafael. 'Rejeneración administrativa fundamental o catástrofe'. Cruz Cárdenas, Antonio, ed. *Grandes oradores colombianos.* (Bogotá: Imprenta Nacional de Colombia, 1997), p. 3. http://www.banrepcultural.org/blaavirtual/indice

Park, James W. *Rafael Núñez and the Politics of Colombian Regionalism, 1863–1886.* (Baton Rouge and London: Louisiana State University Press, 1985).

Paúl, José Telésforo. Bishop of Panama. *Carta Pastoral del Illmo. Sr. Dr. José Telésforo Paúl, Obispo de Panamá, al venerable clero y fieles de su diócesis.* N° 1. (Panamá: Imprenta del *Star and Herald:* Abril de 1876).

Paúl, José Telésforo. *Carta Pastoral de José Telésforo Paúl al venerable clero y fieles de su diócesis.* (Panamá: Imprenta del *Star and Herald,* 1883).

Paúl, José Telésforo. *El Obispo de Panamá al Congreso de Colombia. Exposición que hace el Obispo de Panamá al Congreso de los Estados Unidos de Colombia.* (Bogotá: Imprenta Echeverría y Hermanos, 1878),

Pérez, Manuel José. *Ensayos Morales, Políticos y Literarios.* (Panamá: Imprenta de M. R. de la Torre, 1888).

Porras, Belisario. *Galimatías o Marsías tocando la flauta.* (Panamá: Imprenta de M. R. de la Torre e Hijos, 1891).

Postcard showing the first version of the Panamanian coat of arms (4 June 1905*).* Colección del Museo del Canal Interoceánico de Panamá.

Raat, William D. 'Agustín Aragón and México's Religion of Humanity', *Journal of Inter-American Studies,* V. 11. No. 3. (Miami: Center for Latin American Studies at the University of Miami, July, 1969), p. 441–457. http://www.jstor.org/stable/165422

Sociedad 'El Progreso del Istmo'. Velada literaria en celebración del 28 de noviembre 'Sociedad El Progreso del istmo'. (Panamá: Tipografía de M. R. de la Torre e hijos, 1889).

Soler, Ricaurte. *El Pensamiento político en los siglos XIX y XX.* Soler, Ricaurte, comp. and ed. (Panamá: Universidad de Panamá, 1988).

CHAPTER 3

La Regeneración and the Rise of the Pedagogical Elite in Panama, 1878–1903

After the Constitution of 1886 was promulgated, the Congress of Republic of Colombia met for the first time in 1887. When presenting his *Informe* to the Congress, the Minister of Public Instruction of Colombia, Jesús Casas Rojas, a lawyer and pedagogue, gave a speech loaded with Catholic terminology and imagery. Occasionally, he did use scientific metaphors and concepts, demonstrating how for him, science and religion were not necessarily polar opposites. He began his speech celebrating how Colombia had 'consummated, through the aid of Divine Providence, the most complete transformation from the old federative regime into a unitary republic'.[1] He celebrated that the Constitution of 1886 reincorporated the Catholic religion as a central pillar of education, because it 'carries in its core a principle of vital importance for effective regeneration and good forward movement for the Republic'. Accordingly, this would result in a 'renaissance of good and healthy ideas on education'.[2] In Casas Rojas' speech, the policies of the 'federative regime' had negatively resulted in regression. The fact that the new government officially supported Catholicism was not exactly anything new or unknown, but represented a return to what he imagined as a morally healthier past, from which

---

[1] Jesús Casas Rojas. *Informe Presentado al Congreso de Colombia en su Sesión de 1888.* (Bogotá: unclear publisher, n.d.), p. v.
[2] Ibid.

© The Author(s) 2020
R. de la Guardia Wald, *Education, Conservatism, and the Rise of a Pedagogical Elite in Colombian Panama*,
https://doi.org/10.1007/978-3-030-50046-7_3

Colombia would restart its route towards progress, partly thanks to religious education.

Casas Rojas, like most of his religious peers, seemed to hold paradoxical views on students' nature. On the one hand, their performance was not related to their efforts in study, but on the essence of their soul. In his notable speech, comparing students' future to the supposed predetermined growth of seeds and plants, he argued that several elements were needed to educate children. The educative efforts of parents and teachers were not enough by themselves.

> [Learning] would be inconceivable if the students did not have, deep down in their soul, a certain potency, a certain inexplicable power of thought, of consciousness, and of speech, which arises due from a mysterious impulse that escapes all reason, and this is not the same in all individuals, rather they render diverse fruits, without [any] correlation between the effort [made] and the result [obtained].[3]

Casas Rojas explained how the education system produces different kinds of individuals despite the reading of the same books and receiving the same lectures from the same teachers. Some of them could become 'saints', others might become criminals who brought the 'scandal of their intemperance into the world', wise men with 'invaluable mines of knowledge', the 'sophists that profess and propagate errors', the 'prudent men who save peoples', or the 'demagogues who pervert them'.[4] From this position, he argues that the nature of the students' (intangible) soul determines their future. Knowledge and skills might transform them into leading politicians and professionals, but not necessarily into agents of moral progress. On the other hand, and contradictorily, nature, skills and intelligence were not enough to become a good student. Their destiny must be shaped through hard work or they will become lazy.[5]

Although for Casas Rojas, there was always an essentialist element in his description of students, he claimed that humans are 'born to life with an undeniable germ of concupiscence'.[6] He argued that the teachings of Christ were the only thing that could 'save the souls' and morality of

---

[3] Ibid., p. vii.
[4] Ibid., p. viii.
[5] Ibid.
[6] Ibid., p. xiv.

individuals.[7] According to Rojas, as 'the educator of humanity',[8] Christ not only teaches through the gospel and example but through 'daily works, effectively and directly, upon the father, the mother and the teacher, to whom He has delegated sacred functions'. Yet, for Casas Rojas, Christ also worked directly upon 'children, whose charming innocence He singularly highlighted'.[9] As per the Bible, Rojas believed that even though humans are born with a tendency to fall into temptation, children are innocent. Despite the lack of consistency, it might be possible to infer that, in the Minister's rhetoric, innocence was never completely pure. It was, then, the role of the system of education and teachers to preserve and advance the good spirit of some students; and control the bad spirit of others. This could only be done by mimicking Jesus as an exemplary educator and having a vocation within the precepts of Christian morality.

Casas Rojas' speech illustrates only one of the many discursive variations of the era of conservative hegemony in Colombia. Its foundations, though, demonstrate that conservatives did not reject scientific knowledge as a helpful tool to achieve material progress. Science, however, should not question Catholic beliefs, which were crucial for both the moral rejuvenation and progress of the nation. Because it explained different phenomena in the world, scientific knowledge was, at the same time, a metaphor and a demonstration of God's perfect creation and plan. The Minister of Public Instruction of Colombia construed *La Regeneración* as part of this divine project. Humanity as whole and Colombia particularly had to suffer a process of political and spiritual catharsis to reach order and advancement. Albeit Casas Rojas conceived God as almighty, the plan of regeneration could be endangered by the unsupervised divulgation of scientific and philosophical knowledge. Teachers, more than any other professionals, played a major part in the subjugation of any area of science and philosophy to religion. Their 'apostleship' was described as crucial to orientate Colombia back to a proper moral path. In this sense, Public Instruction, thus, had the mission of teaching the nation's youth to balance out and mix the benefits of science and technology with those of observing Catholic morality as a way to prevent another crisis and to become truly civilised.

[7] Ibid., p. xi.
[8] Ibid., pp. xi–xii.
[9] Ibid., p. xi.

PART I. DISCOURSE AND PEDAGOGICAL DEBATES IN PANAMA DURING *LA REGENERACIÓN* 1876–1903

A study of the dominant discourses of the era serves as a mean to understand the rise of the pedagogical elite, especially because their speeches, writings and reports reflect some of the arguments on education exposed by official political newspapers, and well-established intellectuals and institutions such as the Church. Thus, this section explores the educational discourse of Catholic leaders and periodicals, as well as conservative intellectual, Manuel José Pérez.

The Church: Catholic Views on Pedagogics and Its Informal Educational Practices in the Isthmus

As previously described, during *La Regeneración* the Church was reintroduced to the branch of public instruction in Colombia. In the case of Panama, priests and nuns from different orders, especially Saint Vincent de Paúl, the Brothers of Calasanz, Jesuits and the Brothers of Lasalle controlled several schools. However, the Church intended to extend its influence on educational philosophy and practice via ceremonies, periodicals, public activities, speeches and catechism.

An example of this is Bishop José Telésforno Paúl's Pastoral Letter No. 1 of 1876. There he expressed deep concern about the situation of education under liberal governments all over the world. He wrote:

> Speaking as humans, could it be expected that the world will improve? With the cultivation, and selection of seeds, plants are enhanced, and animals do this through the mixing of breeds and changing of climate. We could expect an improvement for Men, if at least within the decadence of character ... the depression of elevated sentiment ... we take care of the future, [by] preparing a youth fed with Truth, and invigorated with the practice of virtue [i.e. religion].[10]

The comparison between the improvement of plants and animals and humanity seems to refer to a process of selection and exclusion using a sort of scientific practice to choose those who would be morally better in the

---

[10] Paúl, *Carta Pastoral del Illmo. Sr. Dr. José Telésforo Paúl, Obispo de Panamá, al venerable clero y fieles de su diócesis.* N° 1 ..., pp. 3–4.

future. For Paúl, adult members of society were already damaged and difficult to reform. The best option, then, was to support youngsters.

However, the Bishop of Panama was sceptical about the possibility of materialising this goal, because governments all over the world were attempting to own education. Those in power were 'thinking only to instruct' without caring about 'the formation of children's hearts under [the precepts of] Christian morality' or to 'what seems incredible, they try to and do remove the notion of God from schools'.[11] The reason for this, he claimed, was that some of these men perceived this 'severe morality' and 'the memory, name and laws of Jesus Christ' as an obstacle to satisfy 'their frenzy' or libertine impulses. He presupposed that opposition to Catholic education could lead to a moral degeneration among children. They could be filled 'with aversions learned from their teachers which poison the soul with an independent moral doctrine'. Therefore, 'youth grows with no respect and love for anything, adoring themselves, and dreaming of distinctions and pleasures'. This combined with 'ambitions that one would not imagine proper of their tender hearts, unless one had not seen them agitated by passions that would be alarming even in grown men'.[12]

In this text, children and adolescents appear as in Popkewitz's paradox, in which they are both members of society, but also outside of it. Children's souls are still a *tabula rasa*. They are not good or evil. They are shaped by the content you instil in them through teaching. They are compared to plants and animals in the sense that they are not yet masters of their consciousness. So, they still need to be bred, selected and nurtured to become productive adults. For Paúl, though, the problem was that many irreligious governments took education away from the Church, and were already teaching youngsters to celebrate a sort of socially unconscious individualism.

Regarding education programmes, he advised the members of his diocese to teach the children not only to memorise the catechism, but also the history of the Church, so that they could understand its non-perennial labour. He deemed this as the basis of an education that aimed to 'make men moral beings'.[13] It can be said that the Bishop's discourse preached social reform

---

[11] Ibid., p. 4.

[12] Ibid.

[13] José Telésforo Paúl. *Carta Pastoral de José Telésforo Paúl al venerable clero y fieles de su diócesis*. (Panamá: Imprenta del *Star and Herald*, 1883), p. 17.

and pointed out that the teaching of religion to children was necessary to create a moral society. Paúl's view reflects the idea that children needed Christian values to eventually become proper members of society. As Popkewitz stated, the child here is seen as someone outside of society who needs guidance in order to be useful for the community. In addition, the Bishop of Panama's words suggest that children need to learn about the constant search for perfectibility of the Church, so that they can contribute to it through the learning of the catechism.

In 1893, the Diocese of Panama began to publish a bi-weekly periodical called *El Boletín Diocesano* (*The Diocesan Bulletin*). Its content was a potpourri of writings or speeches by the new Bishop José Alejandro Peralta; short hagiographies and stories about religious festivities; news about other parishes in Colombia and the world; reports on the deeds and policies of Pope Leo XIII; publications of old and recent Catholic intellectuals, especially from France and Spain; articles from other Catholic newspapers; prayers and poems; a calendar of patrons saints and martyrs; lists of or explanations on prohibited books; and sections of *Variedades* (miscellaneous local news); and the *Exposición Colectiva del Epicospado Latino-Americano* (The Collective Exposition of the Latin American Episcopate). In addition, it proposed ways to teach or divulge catechism and information about education in Panama and elsewhere.

The leaders of the Church in Panama gave such an importance to the periodical that on 20 November 1893, a letter, 'Circular No. 4', written by educator and Superior Inspector of the Congregation of the Mission of Saint Vincent de Paúl, Tomás Gougnon, requested the Bishop to declare that the *Boletín Diocesano* was the 'official organ' of the *Junta Central Directiva de Enseñanza Catequista* (Directing Central Council for the Teaching of Catechism). *El Boletín Diocesano* divulged information about how the Church illustrated and participated in promoting (formal and informal) religious education.[14]

In addition, the 'Circular No. 4' compelled priests of all parishes in Panama and the secretaries of the parish councils to annually choose six children, three girls and three boys, who had 'distinguished themselves for attending the courses of catechism and their performance'. Similarly, the Junta Central Directiva requested the priest to also list the name of three girls and three boys who have done well in the courses of catechism, and 'excelled in their performance and punctual attendance'. Their names

[14] Tomás Gougnon. Circular No. 4, *El Boletín Diocesano*. Año 1. No. 11 (Panamá: 1 December 1893), p. 86.

were to be published in *El Boletín Diocesano* for 'their own honour, satisfaction of their parents, and the stimulation of others'.[15] The call seemed to have a good reception in the whole Isthmus, as evidenced by the fact that four years later the priests of the parishes of Antón, Tonosí, Macaracas, Chorrera, Natá,[16] Portobelo[17] and Santiago[18] still sent the list of the best students of catechism.

The same edition of this periodical discussed an issue raised by a priest, who consulted about the best way to divulge catechist education in Santiago de Veraguas, where there seemed to be many limitations. The members of the Junta Central Directiva recommended, first, to ask for the cooperation of the Brothers of Saint Vincent de Paúl who had a seat in Veraguas. Moreover, the vice-president of the Junta Directiva suggested that it was convenient to 'propagate among children and persons of the countryside ... little books, brochures, and single pages of propaganda with the end of ingraining in them Christian sentiments and firmly secure [their way] in the healthy and beneficial instructions and learnings that they received during catechism'. Acknowledging this, the vice-president and the Junta Central Directiva had already opted to subscribe to get fifty issues of a Spanish magazine called *La Lectura Popular* (The Popular Reading). The reason for choosing this publication was that its content was 'entertaining and instructive' and dealt with 'the most important religious matters and the most complicated current issues' through short stories while using such a 'simple language that it could be understood even by the most neglected intelligences'.[19] Here is an example of leaders of the Catholic Church attempting to reach the rural population through informal education. Interestingly, there is a separation between children from the countryside and the rest of the rural population. Both are deemed as having underdeveloped intellects. Nonetheless, it seems that children are not yet seen as persons.

The Church also organised ceremonies that involved the students of public schools in religious events unrelated to the curriculum or

[15] Ibid.

[16] 'Catequística', *El Boletín Diocesano*. Año IV. No. 94, Panamá: 1 de marzo de 1897, p. 272.

[17] 'Catequistica', *El Boletín Diocesano*. Año IV. No. 97, Panamá: 15 de junio de 1897, p. 779.

[18] 'Catequística', *El Boletín Diocesano*. Año V. No. 105 , Panamá: 15 de diciembre de 1897, p. 831.

[19] Editorial. 'No title', *El Boletín Diocesano*. Año 1. No. 11 , Panamá: 1 de diciembre de 1893, p. 86.

programmed school activities. For instance, on 22 March 1894, there was the robbery in the Cathedral of Panama. The Bishop Jose Antonio Peralta, addressed the inhabitants of the city to describe the crime. Apparently, the thieves opened the sanctuary and extracted the pyx. This container had piece of communion bread that 'had been kept for the urgent cases that might have occurred during the last three days of Easter'. The Bishop highlighted the stealing of the 'majestic monstrance, which had been gilded a few days before and prepared to be placed on its throne for the occasion of the solemn mass on Easter day'. The thieves were captured and one of them confessed committing the crime. According to the Bishop, the police was still investigating where the sacred pyx was hidden, but the monstrance had been found in a place called 'El Guabo' (a common name used for a kind of tree). It was 'all crushed and broken into pieces, missing most of the cherubs and all the stones of the circles and rays, which, fortunately, were not precious'. This last phrase seemingly lessened the importance of the robbery, yet he insisted on its gravity by saying 'This horrible sacrilege, which so justly has disturbed our heart, has also caused profound indignation on you, beloved children.' The bishop underlined that the robbery had been criticised 'in all the main periodicals of the city', a demonstration that most of the population was outraged. Because there was 'such a general and spontaneous demonstration of religious sentiment', he proposed to make 'an act of solemn piety and faith' at the Cathedral, where 'impious hands dared to affront and vilify the Majesty of the Lord, on the same day when we commemorated the institution of the august Sacrament of the altars'.[20] Hence, on 28 April 1894, Bishop Peralta 'ordered' the organisation of a 'solemn religious event of expiation and amendment to Sacramental Jesus [i.e. the Eucharist]' to happen on 3 May 1894, the day of the Ascent of Christ. The programme consisted on a series of masses from 6 am. Mass of Exposition, two normal masses—after the second of these there was a communion to which the troops stationed at Panama City had to attend—and a pontifical mass. At midday, the Bishop planned a set of chants and prayers. Later, at 5 pm, the attendants went on a procession with stations at the five altars, after which they would receive a blessing at 6 pm. Then the programme stated that students of different schools would visit the '*Santísimo*' (the holiest Lord) at the Cathedral taking turns in the following order: Colegio Balboa; the

[20] José Antonio Peralta, Bishop of Panama, 'El Obispo de Panamá al pueblo católico de la Ciudad', *El Boletín Diocesano*. Año I No. 20, Panamá, 1 de mayo de 1894, p. 164.

Internado de la Sagrada Familia (the boarding students of the School of the Holy Family); the Externado de la Sagrada Familia (the non-boarding students of the School of the Holy Family); Las Huérfanas de Santo Tomás (the Orphans of Saint Thomas); Las Huérfanas de San José (the Orphans of Saint Joseph); La Escuela de la Fe (the School of Faith); Escuela de Varones de Santa Ana (the All-Boys' School of Santa Ana); Escuela de Niñas de Santa Ana (the All-Girls' School of Santa Ana); Escuela Anexa del Colegio Balboa (the Annexed School of the Colegio Balboa); and the Schools ruled by Mrs Ucrós, Bastar and Alvarado.[21] Additionally, the students of the Seminary were allowed to enter the Cathedral in pairs.[22] Finally, the Bishop exhorted the people of Panama City to 'pay a visit, with all piety and reserve, to Sacramented Jesus' during the day. He also indicated that over the next few days there would be a charity collection to acquire a new monstrance. 'For each of these acts of religious piety, we will concede forty days of true indulgence',[23] he finished. The prize the Bishop offered to those who participated in the act of exculpation, 'forty days of true indulgence', indicates that spiritual rewards and believe in purification were appreciated by a significant number of the people of the capital.

The Bishop's letter also implies that the whole of Panamanian society needed redemption in order to be purified. Even though the robbers were just a few people, all the community had to request Jesus's pardon. That is, the sins of the few extended to the rest of the population. In spite of that, supposedly, most of Panama City's population was outraged and showed serious Catholic spirit, for Peralta this was not enough. Thus, the organisation of a major event took place to expiate the inhabitants of the capital city. The fact that most of the major public and private schools were involved in the events illustrates how, by 1894, the Church shaped Panamanian education from outside and within the offices of the Ministry of Public Instruction, the Government of the Department of Panama and schools. Moreover, it shows the vision that the Bishop and his advisors had of children and students. As with all the inhabitants of Panama City, the children and students needed to participate in the event to strengthen their respect for the authority, symbols and values of the Catholic Church. For students this was mandatory, which suggests that they were seen as a potential danger to the Church and Catholicism. If they were not cleansed in the present, they would be

[21] Ibid.
[22] Ibid.
[23] Ibid.

more inclined to sin in the future. The question arises over a possible connection between the obligatory engagement of schools and the age of the actual thieves. Whether the latter were youngsters or not might explain why students were compulsorily included in the events.

There were, nonetheless, divided opinions about the results of the work of religious orders in the promotion of Christianity in Colombian Panama. Religious orders' social services and charitable actions were, apparently, mostly appreciated. For example, the role of the Nuns of Charity of Saint Vincent de Paúl's managing of the Asilo de Niñas was admired by many. The teacher was Mr Patricio Meneses, a graduate from the *Escuela Normal de Varones*. The institution even had its own *Revista del Asilo de Niñas*, edited by locally renowned writer from the *Arrabal*, Federico Escobar, and administered by benefactor Manuel Jaén, father of a girl who died in Jamaica. This periodical contained readings addressed to the donors and the orphan girls, which were loaded with religious teachings and notions on theoretical and practical education,[24] as well as nationalist messages. These were sometimes conveyed in short essays, poems and letters.[25] In 1890, a satisfied General Inspector of Public Instruction of Panama, José Agustín Torres, congratulated the role of the *Hermanas de la Caridad* (Sisters of Charity) for their work in promoting 'Christian sentiment' in the student body and requested the Departmental and National Governments to support them legally and financially.[26] In contrast, the same year, the report of vice-rector of the Seminary of Panama to the General Inspector of Public Instruction complained that the seminary only had fourteen students.[27] This might entail that the inhabitants of

---

[24] Juvenal, (pseudonym). 'Teoría y Práctica', *Revista del Asilo de Niñas*. Panamá: Imprenta de Samuel N. Ramos, 1 de marzo de 1892, no pages.

[25] *Revista del Asilo de Niñas*. No. 22 Año 2. and No. 39 Año 3, Panamá: Imprenta de Samuel N. Ramos, 1 de marzo de 1892– 1 de julio de 1893.

[26] Informe del Inspector General de Instrucción Pública de Panamá—República de Colombia—Departamento de Panamá—Inspección General de Instrucción Pública—No. 55—Panamá, 5 de marzo de 1890 in *Informe que el Ministro de Instrucción Pública presenta al Congreso de Colombia en sus sesiones de 1890*. (Bogotá: Imprenta de 'La Luz', 1890), pp. 135–136

[27] Baldomedo Carles V. *Informe del Rector del Seminario de Panamá. Rectorado del Seminario—Sección 9*—*Numero 4, Informe que el Ministro de Instrucción Pública presenta al Congreso de Colombia en sus sesiones de 1890*. (Bogotá: Imprenta de 'La Luz, 3 de julio de 1890), p. 298.

Panama applauded the educational work of Catholic orders, but that Catholic devotion among them was not strong enough to made priest-hood an appealing career.

Manuel José Pérez's Moral Paradoxes: Egalitarian Practical Education and Elitists Projects of Abjections

While establishing his theory on instincts and on antagonism to 'material-ism' in his essay, 'Estudios Morales: El Hombre' (Moral Studies: Mankind), Manuel José Pérez presented the foundations for his moral thoughts on education. After recognising that 'fortunately there was no lack of people with unquestionable competence' in the area of education, the goal of his writings was to 'present a vast field to [human] imagination for the exer-cise of the sacred ministry of instruction and for instilling morality in the peoples'.[28] He was asking his readers to imagine a future when the apostle-ship of educators implanted Christian religion as the main foundation of universal society.

Pérez argued against scientific discourses that defined human beings as another kind of animal. He wrote that it is 'undeniable that mankind is a combination of aberrations', but that it could not be admitted that human-kind had just barely surpassed animal instincts. For him, humans were only similar to the 'irrationals' in their search to satisfy physical needs such as hunger and thirst. In contrast, he added, humankind was different due to its 'affective sentiments, called, as well, sentiments of the heart'. These feelings 'comprehend all the psychological actions that are to a certain point independent from reason and that separate us ... from matter'. For Pérez, two kinds of instincts existed. Some are related to material needs; others are spiritual. By defining them as 'psychological acts', he guided the reader to a scientific analysis of the soul. In this sense, those sentimental instincts are not to be confused with conscious cognition, but they are crucial for differentiating animals from humans.

However, Pérez stated that instincts could be 'exaggerated' and trans-formed into passions. These, he added, 'as their etymology suggests, [pas-sions] make us be in pain'. For him, these led to unreasonable and inconstant behaviour. Pérez concluded that these actions were all 'phe-nomena of the soul' related to the intensification of its 'most noble

---

[28] Manuel José Pérez. 'Estudios Morales: El Hombre', *Ensayos Morales, Políticos y Literarios.* (Panamá: Imprenta de M. R. de la Torre, 1888), p. 1.

faculties, which degenerate into tempestuous passions like hurricanes'.[29] Manuel José Pérez demanded both a moral education of the basic instincts and an education of the sentiments. Since instincts escaped consciousness, humankind required a 'moral education which tends to vivify the soul, and calls it to judge of our own actions, and regulate [our instincts] by drawing the limits within which they have to be constrained so that they do not deviate'.[30] Instructing reason was not enough for releasing humankind from suffering. The actual way to keep humankind away from pain was in providing a moral education that taught the soul to control excessive materialism and to prevent instincts from transforming into passions. This is a 'salvation story of education' which appears as a means to create a virtuous cycle of continuous material and moral progress.

Pérez further developed his ideas on education in 'Ideas Perdidas' (Lost Ideas), so he focused on the issue of practical education. If society is 'an association of individuals who know their duties and rights, the education of those individuals undoubtedly forms the base of that society'. He claimed that the main cause of the backwardness of 'our populations' was a legacy of the 'deficient education that the Spaniards left us'. He argued that Spaniards 'considered working and any profitable occupation as denigrating and unworthy of an hidalgo'.[31] He stressed that Colombians, Panamanians and possibly all Spanish Americans should be 'making reforms and innovations that are imperatively demanded by the advancements and necessities of this era'.[32] Unlike other Spanish American intellectuals, Pérez's comments on the colonial legacies left by Spain and the lack of opportunities and mediocrity of professionals was not related to racial degeneration.[33] Instead, he presented two factors as the cause of mediocrity. On one side, there were inherent human limitations. Not everyone could be a genius. On the other side, it was a cultural issue that could be overcome, as the Spaniards had done.[34]

He added that in Colombian schools there was no care for providing 'children with a practical education, either in the science or the arts ... [for

---

[29] Ibid., pp. 4–5.

[30] Manuel José Pérez, 'El Hombre', *Ensayos* ..., p. 4.

[31] Ibid.

[32] Ibid.

[33] For more on this degeneration theory, racial pessimism and *latinidad* in Spanish America in between the 1880s and 1920, see: Michela Coletta. *Decadent Modernity. Civilization and 'Latinidad' in Spanish America, 1880–1920.* (Liverpool: Liverpool University Press, 2018).

[34] Manuel José Pérez. 'Ideas Perdidas', *Ensayos* ..., p. 26.

which] we have no schools'.[35] Hence, not only in Colombia, but in all Spanish America everyone wanted to be *literatos* (i.e., men of letters), lawyers or businessmen, disregarding whether the person had the capacity to learn, or whether an individual actually had the ability to perform well in a given career. Pérez stated that an inclination for a career was 'not enough to believe that we have the inspiration and the genius to excel in them.' In the same line as Casas Rojas, he continued by writing that 'genius is a wonderful spark that makes some men a sort of lighthouse that enlightens humanity, it is a gift from heaven that is conceded only to a few'. Not everyone could attain it, in spited of how much effort was made.[36] Considering these human limitations, instead of obtaining 'fame', the text posited that those businessmen, lawyers, doctors, and men and women of letters 'would die of hunger' even if they had a degree, because they were 'mediocre'. Even when admitting that 'amongst us, there are those who have deep knowledges in some of [those] fields', he asserted that the Americas (i.e., Spanish America) were 'not yet a convenient theatre for those kinds of professions.'[37]

Change could be achieved by reforming education. 'The noticeable difference between the Latin and Saxon races', he wrote, 'without a doubt is due to the different educational systems'.[38] The 'Saxon' system provided practical education in different arts and crafts. Following this thought, as a solution for this cultural problem that stagnated productivity in Spanish America, Pérez repeated his support for providing a 'practical education, even by force if it was possible, for the sons of the wealthy as for the [sons of the] day labourer'.[39] For him, the creation of Schools of Arts and Crafts was needed, so that children could attain knowledge in an area for which they had an 'inclination'. Nevertheless, this 'inclination' had to be deeply studied by the teachers.[40] The idea of forcing 'practical education' upon children (and parents) who belong to different levels of the social hierarchy appear as quite revolutionary, egalitarian and humbling. He noticed that his ideas would be rejected by parents who cared about their social image. Hence, he tried to convince them that their status would not be

---

[35] Ibid.
[36] Ibid., p. 26.
[37] Ibid.
[38] Ibid., p. 27.
[39] Ibid., p. 26.
[40] Ibid., pp. 26–27.

damaged, because it was a modern and, therefore, a civilised course of action. In this sense, Pérez recommended 'parents who want good for their sons' must be 'exempt of stale preoccupations' and endeavour to 'educate their children according to the ideas of this century'. Doing this, he added, should not and did not affect their 'clean lineage' or become an obstacle to present themselves to good society.'[41]

More importantly, practical of education should fall within the social and moral discourse of Catholicism. Children's 'inclinations' had to be studied and determined by the teachers, not the students. This perspective transpires in his complaint about laws for creating schools that had been 'buried in the archives as food for moths', so that children who wanted or have to learn a craft still needed to become apprentices in an artisans workshop, where they would be 'a servant of the master' or are 'unwatched'. There, they learn empirically but do not even get 'theoretical rudiments'. Besides, they are 'exposed to becoming corrupt' together with the other children, because they have 'absolute liberty' and do not have 'the kind respect [for authority] that only schools can impose'.[42] So, formal 'practical education' was required to make sure students actually learned all aspects of an art or a craft. Equally important, though, was the role of schools in reinforcing respect and prevent children from falling into corruption and becoming a threat to society. Pérez's views on the formalisation of 'practical education' in arts and crafts school was, at the same time, egalitarian and elitist. Everyone should receive the same kind of knowledge in the same school, but this process of learning in such a formal and regulated school gave students a status neglected to those who received a more empirical and traditional training.

Perez's conservatism appears more tangible in his writings on political ideas. In his short essay called *Los Derechos y Deberes de los Pueblos* (The Rights and Duties of the Peoples), he said, that 'politically speaking' the meaning of 'rights' should be: 'the exercise of the faculties granted by the laws'; the definition for 'duties' should be 'the obligations that emanate from the Law'. After indicating that savage people do not know either rights or duties but only force as the 'supreme law', he added that the emergence of the 'idea of Justice engendered Law, and this in turn

---

[41] Ibid.
[42] Ibid., p. 27.

[produced] duties'.[43] He argued that the notion of justice when 'the sentiment of goodness, innate to the heart of Mankind, began to awaken [after entering in] contact with their equals, [and] with the creation of material needs ... that imposed upon them an irresistible force; and with the [creation of] those that had a superfluous appearance, [but] become indispensable, depending on [a society's] degree of civilisation'.[44] In short, as humankind progressed towards the satisfaction of material and spiritual needs and became more civilised, justice replaced force. Human beings began to conceive the 'respect for the rights of others as a guarantee of their own'. Perez added that societies 'rushed ... to normalise' this acknowledgement. He advocated for a balanced relation between rights and duties. Duties prevented the 'abuse' of rights. 'Harmonious' governance was founded on the observation of this principle.

Like many thinkers, and particularly the supporters of *La Regeneración*, Pérez argued that wanting to obtain rights without the imposition of duties would be like wanting to 'craze society, transforming it into a battlefield'. He added that a society in which all members want everything without giving anything away, is doomed to 'regress towards the times of barbarity'.[45] Perez's arguments remind of the conservative motto 'Liberty within Justice'. The diagnostic that unmonitored freedom will result in a chaotic society that will become a 'battlefield' invokes indirectly to the notion that order is needed to reach 'scientific peace' and, of course, progress. In case the contrary happens, for Perez, all the advancement brought about by the development of the idea of justice could disappear if duties were prescribed; instead, there will be a return to the time when the use of force was the means of ruling.

After introducing his main points, Perez passed on to criticise the 'efforts of the Commune and of Nihilism' to create societies without duties. It is not clear whether he was referring to the Paris Commune specifically or to Communism in general, but he posits that the manner in which society is organised implies that 'it could not tolerate the disturbance of laws that guarantee property as the fruit of work'. He continued and stated that his contemporary society 'would aspire to excuse itself

[43] Manuel José Pérez. 'Los Derechos y Deberes de los Pueblos', *Ensayos Morales, Políticos y Literarios*. (Panamá: Imprenta de M. R. de la Torre, 1888), p. 139.
[44] Ibid.
[45] Ibid.

from the fulfilment of the healthy duties that [owning property] demands'.[46] He indicated that this was the path marked by civilization and by 'the necessities of the peoples'. So, it would be a 'crime' to '[o]ffer the unwary a paradise, without telling them that one cannot arrive there but through expiation and sacrifice …'.[47] After comparing the peoples to 'big children', he advised to speak 'the truth' to them. 'If the path they must walk in is covered with thorns instead of flowers, they should know it just like that', he wrote. The purpose of this was to educate them, as 'big children', and to compel them to 'move the soles of their feet away from [the thorns]'. He warned those who lied that, eventually, the peoples will 'curse them for their tortuous behaviour'. He affirmed that these 'curses sometimes become horrible tragedies' and remembered that 'we have witnessed some of them in our republics'.[48]

In Perez's view, all ideologies proposed egalitarianism through the elimination of the existing social order, because they were lies. It was only through an established process of purification and sacrifice, including 'hard work', that people could deserve liberty and property. For him, those false utopias were an invitation to think the contrary, but reality would awaken the peoples. This could not only result in disillusionment, but also in disorder and violence. His comparison of 'peoples' with 'big children' somewhat differs from the vision of childhood proposed by Popkewitz. In this case, it is mostly adults, who belong to the 'peoples', who are projected into the image of children. They are immature and need guidance and knowledge of the truth to prevent them from damaging themselves or others. In short, 'the people' need constant supervision so that they do not derail and endanger the established Catholic and conservative visions of the 'cosmopolitan reason'.

As seen, Pérez was a defender of the posture that populations needed to be controlled, supervised and educated. This view comes out clearer through his opinions on suffrage. He indicated that it was a good example of how duties and right complement each other. After that statement, he explained that suffrage was a right because the peoples should have the faculty to choose the most 'dignified' person to make the laws and 'serve their interests with patriotism, honesty and loyalty'. However, Pérez emphasised why suffrage was a duty. First, 'abstaining from exercising [it]

[46] Ibid., p. 140.
[47] Ibid.
[48] Ibid.

was 'criminal', because it gave free way to 'ambitious' and 'turbulent' men to 'disturb everything', and, as a consequence, 'anarchy would implant its dominion on society'. For him, practicing the duty of suffrage served for the 'conversation of order through the election of the most honourable citizens for public offices'.[49] Not voting would be irresponsible, because problematic and immoderately ambitious people could take advantage and take power and cause disorder. Yet the defence of the selection of the 'most honourable' candidates suggests an elitist approach to suffrage. Order could only be sustained by them. Actually, Pérez expressed his opposition to universal suffrage:

> Unfortunately, [universal suffrage] is a chimera, not only among us [Spanish Americans], but even among advantaged peoples such as the United States, England, France ... Popular elections are always the fruit of the intrigues of *caudillos*, who take advantage of the ignorant masses, making them ever more stupid to achieve their ends. Men of great talent and philanthropical sentiments ... have not slept seeking a solution to such a difficult problem; and no others have shown up to their imagination, but the education of the masses to transform them into people.[50]

This proposition implies a conscious process of exclusion. For Pérez, only the already educated or those who become educated are, respectively, part of or can join 'the people'. It is not clear if there is certain contradiction in the text, for it seems that in previous paragraphs the 'people' or 'big children' did include the 'ignorant masses'. Even amongst this selective group of educated persons, there were hierarchies. The 'most honourable' were to lead the other part of 'the people'. The 'ignorant masses' are dehumanised or at least they still lived in the times of barbarity. Human unity through science and reason could only be achieved if all received an education, but, of course, this had to follow conservative and Catholic precepts, a factor that reinforces the process of exclusion. It was not only until all members of the masses acquired this kind of education to avoid being manipulated that they could become 'people' and have the right and duty of suffrage.

In the meantime, for Pérez, it was immoral to call 'people' those who were uneducated and had little comprehension of rights and duties, as well as what their purposes were in the world. This, however, was 'very

---

[49] Ibid.
[50] Ibid., pp. 140–141.

convenient for those who need to clutter ballots in the electoral urns'. For this reason, he added that within some civilised societies a person 'cannot be an elector without knowing to how to write or read'. For him this were not retrograde ideas: they pointed at what is 'rational and just'. Then he asked why, if societies prefer quality over quantity, it should be desirable that the 'ignorant masses' impose themselves over the 'true people, that is, the part [of the population] that feels and thinks'.[51] Therefore, he exhorted his readers to

> educate the masses, so that they can know what is wanted from them, and so that they judge with their own criteria about the convenience or inconvenience of their actions. In that way, they will not represent, as it is seen every day, the fable of the mutton of Panurge.[52]

Order and proper selection of governors required an education that informed good criteria and permitted these previous members of the masses and new members of 'the peoples' to judge as individuals and without supervision, about the best way to proceed in society and politics. If not, they would remain ignorant, and would follow any *caudillo* blindly as the herd of mutton or sheep of Panurge (a character from *The Life of Gargantua and of Pantagruel*), followed other sheep into the sea, a metaphor for nothingness and death.

PART II. THE BIRTH OF THE PEDAGOGICAL ELITE

Representatives of *La Regeneración* did not limit their projects simply to essays, speeches and newspapers promoting the goals and exalting the achievements of the political reform. They named their supporters in key positions. This extended to local authorities of public instruction in the Department of Panama. There was a group of pedagogues selected to be in charge of realising *La Regeneración*'s visions for collective education by means of designing and implementing the curriculum, creating course content, choosing the most adequate pedagogical techniques to transmit knowledge, applying the pre-emptive and correctional methods to control corruption of teachers and students, and to enact the relevant adjustments to progress and secure modern education.

---

[51] Ibid., p. 141.
[52] Ibid.

Those teachers and professionals chosen to deliver this service to the state became the pedagogical elite. This was not a homogeneous group. There were hierarchies, social differences and professional distinctions. So, as indicated above, many of them were priests who, probably, had worked in the field of education; others were scientists, engineers and lawyers, many of whom had dedicated their lives to teaching; but, the basis of this elite were graduated and professional pedagogues, who slowly replaced and removed other professionals and even priests from schools. Via their connections with the social and political elites, and their intellectual and cultural capital, this pedagogical elite managed to attain high positions not only within the educational system (teachers, rectors and vice-rectors of schools and universities, provincial inspectors; and the highest position, director, general inspector or secretary of public instruction), but also in other sections of the government, as diplomats and legislators. Some even took office as president of Panama.

The Origins: Manuel José Hurtado

Manuel José Hurtado was born in Panama on 1 December 1821. Because his father José Manuel had written and signed Panama City's Declaration of Independence from Spain three days before he was born, Manuel José wrote in his will: 'I was the first person born in this city at the moment of swearing allegiance to independence from Spain.'[53] Between 1824 and 1828, his father was Ambassador of Colombia in London, so Hurtado spent part of his childhood in Great Britain and France.[54] In 1834, his father also became governor of the Isthmus, but returned to Europe in 1836.[55] Because of this, Hurtado received a European education. He first studied in London, but then went on to study civil engineering in Paris.[56] Hurtado returned to Panama in 1847 and attempted to work in his profession. However, like many of his peers in Colombia, he was not able to find employment due to the country's lack of financial and technological

---

[53] Manuel José Hurtado. 'Testamento', cited in Juan Antonio Susto, 'Manuel José Hurtado, fundador de la Instrucción Pública en el Istmo', *Revista Lotería* N° 55 (Panamá: Diciembre, 1945), p. 9.

[54] Juan Antonio Susto, 'Manuel José Hurtado, fundador de la Instrucción Pública en el Istmo', *Revista Lotería* N° 55 (Panamá: Diciembre, 1945), p. 18.

[55] Ibid., p. 20.

[56] Ibid., p. 22.

resources as well as its political instability.[57] As an alternative, he tried to initiate a political career.[58] But like many nineteenth-century Colombian and Panamanian engineers and scientists, Hurtado ended up helping to develop public education as previously explained.[59]

It is difficult to know whether Hurtado defended liberal and conservative views. This is partly because politicians and biographers appropriated his persona for one of the existing political parties. This was a tool to illustrate their collective's commitment to education. On the one side, Hurtado's father served as Governor of Panama under the government of Francisco de Paúla Santander (1832–1837), whose followers supposedly founded the Liberal Party in 1848. Hurtado himself collaborated with *Liberales Radicales*, such as Buenaventura Correoso (1868–1871 and 1878–1879), until the beginning of *La Regeneración*. However, there is also evidence that Hurtado might have been a conservative or was a moderate liberal or even transformed into a conservatised *Liberal Independiente*. First, his father was a monarchist.[60] Second, some newspapers, such the conservative *El Aliento*, claimed that Hurtado was a Conservative.[61] Third, many of the students and colleagues who studied or worked in the *Escuela Normal de Institutores*, such as Nicolás Pacheco, Nicolas Victoria Jaén, Mélchor Lasso de la Vega or Valentín Bravo, became leading educators during *La Regeneración* and continued being pedagogical authorities under the conservative-led Panamanian governments established after the secession from Colombia in 1903.[62]

The fact is that he did advocate for the professionalisation of education. One of the few references found to Hurtado's writings is a text called 'La profesión de maestro' ('The Teacher's Profession'), which alludes to the poor preparation of teachers, practical education and the lack of parental interest in sending their children to school.[63] This was a defence of the professionalisation of teaching as a key step towards progress. It was a call to teachers and students of the *Escuela Normal*, who could see this as an

[57] Safford, *The Ideal of the Practical...*, p. 162.
[58] Susto and Eliet, p. 22.
[59] Ibid., p. 28. For similar cases in Colombia: Safford. *The Ideal of the Practical...*, pp. 161–162.
[60] Eliet and Susto, p. 58.
[61] Editorial. '¿Se Amostazan?'. *El Aliento. Político, Noticioso y de Variedades*. Serie I, N° 2. Panamá: enero 30 de 1891, p. 2.
[62] Bernal, p. 53.
[63] Manuel José Hurtado. 'La profesión de maestro' in Céspedes, pp. 199–200.

attempt to protect their careers and futures. For teachers, Hurtado was a modern-day role model and demonstrable tamer of students; whilst, for students, he personified a successful individual and encapsulated a professional future. In Bourdieu's words, he would appear as a transformer of social spaces and *habitus*, that is, as a life-changer.

Social Spaces and the Escuela Normal de Varones

There is scarce information about the personal relations between the directors and graduates of the *Escuela Normal* de Varones, governmental and ecclesiastical authorities, and social and political leaders. Following Bourdieu's theory, many directors and graduates belonged to or entered the social spaces and acquired *habitus* of some of the authorities of *La Regeneración* and the established elites. Looking at lists of its directors and its fifty-six graduates from 1874 to 1884 (see Annex 2) leads one to think that it was at the *Escuela Normal* de Varones where most of these pedagogues acquired the cultural capital that allowed them into new social spaces.[64]

This school was founded in 1872, during the time of Liberal dominance. Its first director was Oswald Wirsing, one of the nine Germans pedagogues recruited by the *Liberales Radicales'* government to strengthen teacher training.[65] This was also the time when pedagogical debates regarding the teaching of religion and the use of certain textbooks in Colombian schools led to the previously mentioned War of the Books or Civil War of 1876–1877. Considering Frank Safford's remark on how conservative parents avoided sending their children to public school to prevent them from absorbing liberal ideas or being taught under the directorship of liberal laic or protestant pedagogues,[66] it is likely that wealthy conservative adolescents did not attend this school. However, it is important to take into account that most students did not seem to belong to the wealthiest families in Panama. Most of them were from the countryside: forty-six were either from cities and towns in the Provinces of Coclé, Colón, Los Santos and Chiriquí or from towns in the Province of Panama. Only ten were from Panama City.[67] The fact that many of the

[64] Ernesto J. Castillero R. and Juan Antonio Susto. *Panameños Ilustres: El Maestro Don Nicolás Pacheco. Símbolo del Magisterio Nacional (1853–1924).* (Panamá: Imprenta Nacional, 1953), pp. 25–32.

[65] Bosco Bernal, p. 53.

[66] Safford, *Ideal of the Practical* ..., p. 162.

[67] Castillero Reyes and Susto. *Panameños Ilustres: El maestro Don Nicolás Pacheco* ..., pp. 24–25.

students were siblings or otherwise related as they had the same surname and were from the same town (as are the cases of Manuel C. Jurado and Salvador Jurado from David in the Province of Chiriquí and Aurelio Guardia and Carlos Guardia from San Carlos in the Province of Panama) suggests that they or their parents might have disregarded ideology and beliefs to give priority to personal or family necessities that a professional career as teachers would satisfy.

Little is known about Oswald Wirsing, except for the fact that he stopped being director in 1879. There is no information about his possible departure from, or death in Panama. This year coincides, though, with Manuel José Hurtado's resignation and the beginning of *La Regeneración*. Presumably, he was adept to his Liberal recruiters and employers, but there is no information about his ideology and social practices, and, consequently, about his connections to social and political elites. So, it is difficult to point out to what extent ideological or political input had on the students, nor it is possible to know if Wirsing had strong connections with social and political authorities to help students to rise as members of the pedagogical elite. So far, what can be said is that many prominent educators graduated under Wirsing's directorship. These are the cases of Nicolás Pacheco and Simeón Conte (from Penonomé in the Province of Coclé). Besides this, Pacheco and other two students, Liberato Trujillo and Nemesio Pérez, obtained the highest degree of superior or secondary schoolteacher while Wirsing ruled the school.[68] Trujillo and conservative Conte[69] would become school directors and inspectors, while Pacheco became director of the *Escuela Normal*.

After Valentín Bravo, who had been sub-director under Wirsing, took control of the school in 1880, more connections seem clearer. Judging from the fact that his sons, Manuel and Abel, got excellent positions working for the Church or within the educational system under *La Regeneración*, Bravo was a either a conservative or a conservatised-liberal. He lasted one year in the position. His successor was Adolfo Fernández, who, as mentioned before, was a *Liberal Independiente* and supporter of Pablo Arosemena's candidacy in 1882. Fernández directed the school from

[68] Ernesto J. Castillero R. and Juan Antonio Susto. *Panameños Ilustres: El Maestro Don Nicolás Pacheco. Símbolo del Magisterio Nacional (1853–1924)*. (Panamá: Imprenta Nacional, 1953), p. 24.
[69] Simeón Conte. 'Dos Palabras', *El Sufragio*. N° 2 Panamá: Tipografía Torre e hijos, 30 de mayo de 1891, p. 4.

1881 to 1883, a period when the prevalence of graduates from the countryside began to rise. In three years, only one out of the sixteen graduates was from Panama City. Among these graduates, there were three new secondary schoolteachers from the Province of Coclé: Pacífico Tapia (Aguadulce), Eliseo Martínez (Penonomé) and Nicolás Victoria Jaén (Aguadulce).[70] Tapia and Martínez became inspectors of Public Instruction. Victoria Jaén was openly a conservative and participated in the scenario of political polemics.[71] Furthermore, he rose to the charge of Secretary of Public Instruction of the Republic of Panama after 1903.[72]

As said, Nicolás Pacheco, a former student of the *Escuela Normal de Varones*, stepped up to direct the school from 1883 to 1884. More will be said about Pacheco later. Here it is worth mentioning that there were nine graduates from the countryside and only one from Panama City.[73] Melchor Lasso de la Vega from Aguadulce, another main member of the pedagogical elite, was one of these graduates.

The Discourse, Practices and Work of the Pedagogical Elite

As Kirkendall argues, education produced the configuration of an exclusive student community, which perceived itself as having authority over the rest of the population 'by linking access to education ... to access to political life'. Nevertheless not all of the Isthmian pedagogical elite 'enhanced the legitimacy of existing authority by giving an oligarchy the added appearance of seeming to be a meritocracy'.[74] This is the case of those teachers who did not belong to the 'oligarchy' or form part of the 'existing authority', but joined those social and political spheres. They did enhance the legitimacy of those with authority, but they also needed to demonstrate or, at least, pretend that they had earned their status.

The members of the pedagogical elite acquired a kind of cultural capital that allowed them to show both possession of the ability to reproduce the

---

[70] Ibid., pp. 25–32.
[71] Rodolfo Aguilera. *Galería de Hombres Públicos del Istmo*. (Panamá: Tipografía de Casís y Cia, 1906), p. 50.
[72] Ibid.
[73] Ernesto J. Castillero R. and Juan Antonio Susto. *Nicolás Pacheco* ... pp. 31–32.
[74] Andrew J. Kirkendall. 'Student Culture and Nation-State Formation', *Beyond Imagined Communities. Reading and Writing the Nation in Nineteenth-Century Latin America*. John Charles Chasteen and Sara Castro-Klarén, eds. (Washington, D.C., Baltimore and London: Woodrow Wilson Center Press—The Johns Hopkins University Press, 2003), p. 9.

dominant political language and the pedagogical knowledge that would allow them to practice teaching techniques that would effectively promote the principles of *La Regenereción*. That is, their speeches, writings, courses, curricula design, school inspections, reports and lessons ensured religious education, the instilment of conservative views on order and progress, and the related approaches to technical or scientific instruction. As examples there are the reports, publications and speeches of Melchor Lasso de la Vega and Abel Bravo, as well as the use of official periodicals, such as *Reseña Escolar*, to promote their own deeds and conservative governance.

The First Graduate: Nicolás Pacheco (1853–1924)

The life of Nicolas Pacheco illustrates the connection between Hurtado, the *Escuela Normal de Varones*, its graduates, the pedagogical elite, the Church, and the State. First, it is important to mention that Pacheco's graduation examiners were Manuel José Hurtado and two priests, including the future Bishop of Panama and Archbishop of Colombia, José Telésforo Paúl.[75] After he graduated from the *Escuela Normal* in 1874, he began as a Director of an All-Mens' Elementary School of Santa Ana.[76] He stayed in that position for thirty-eight years[77] and received a recognition from the government in 1882.[78] This did not impede him from taking the position of Secretary of the Directorship of Public Instruction in 1875.[79] He thus worked directly for Manuel José Hurtado. Moreover, as indicated, he also ruled the *Escuela Normal de Varones* from 1883 to 1885. Pacheco, apparently, was an avid contributor to the pages of *Reseña Escolar* from 1888 to 1908,[80] a detail that suggests that his writings were approved by the conservative and *liberal independiente* authorities and editors of the periodical. With the consolidation of *La Regeneración*, Pacheco founded an ephemeral private school that followed the model of a teachers' school, El Colegio de la Razón.[81] Also, he appears as teacher and rector of the All-

---

[75] Ernesto J. Castillero R. and Juan Antonio Susto. *Nicolás Pacheco ...*), p. 22.
[76] Ibid., pp. 33–34.
[77] Ibid., p. 36.
[78] Ibid., pp. 39–40.
[79] Ibid., p. 36.
[80] Ibid., p. 37.
[81] Nicolas Pacheco. 'Informe Colegio Superior de la Razón al Inspector General de Instrucción Pública del Departamento de Panamá' in Ministerio de Instrucción Pública. *Informe presentado al Congres de la República en sus Ordinarias de 1888 por el Ministro de Instrucción Pública*. (Bogotá: Imprenta de la 'Luz', 1888), p. 77.

Men Elementary School of San Felipe, a school annexed to the Colegio Balboa ruled by Abel Bravo.[82] Although his career was not as successful as those who followed after, it shows that studying pedagogics and becoming a teacher could help establish strong links with members of the elites and persons in high institutional positions. Consequently, it could also lead to the obtainment of influential positions within the field of education. Pacheco's story is one of becoming tamed by the educational system, of attaining new cultural capital and changing social spaces and *habitus*. From a very practical viewpoint, at least, doing this could help people to mobilise both socially and politically.

Technical Reports for the Sake of Regeneration and Morality: Abel Bravo (1861–1934)

Valentín Bravo, one of the directors of the *Escuela Normal de Varones*, had three sons: Manuel Valentín, Enrique and Abel. There is not much information about Manuel Valentín and Enrique, but it is known that the former went into teaching in schools, most notably at the Colegio Balboa. Although one of his biographies lamented that his achievements have not been truly recognised because of his conservatism,[83] Abel had a relatively more famous career. According to the same biographer, he was a student of Oswald Wirsing and José Telésforo Paúl.[84] It seems that he enrolled at the *Escuela Normal de Varones*. In 1878, at the age of seventeen, he was named professor of mathematics at the recently founded *Escuela Normal de Señoritas*. When he turned twenty-one, the government of the Sovereign State of Panama named him bookkeeper. Soon after, Bishop José Telesforo Paúl contracted him to teach at the Seminary.[85] In 1881, he travelled to Bogotá, where he enrolled at the Escuela de Ingeniería Civil y Militar de

[82] Abel Bravo. *Informe del Colegio Balboa*. República de Colombia—Departamento de Panamá—Colegio Balboa—Rectoría—Numero 8—Panamá, Abril 24 de 1890, *Informe que el Ministro de Instrucción Pública presenta al Congreso de Colombia en sus sesiones de 1890*. (Bogotá: Imprenta de 'La Luz', 1890), p. 295.

[83] Diógenes Cedeño Cenci (?), Sociedad de Geográfica de Colombia and Academia de Ciencias Geográficas. 'Rasgos Biográficos de Don Abel Bravo (1861–1934)' in *Artículo del Boletín de la Sociedad de Geográfica de Colombia*. No. 77–78. Vol. XXI (Bogotá: Sociedad de Geográfica de Colombia, 1963), p. 4. https://www.sogeocol.edu.co/documentos/078_rasg_bio_abel_bravo.pdf

[84] Ibid., p. 2.

[85] Aguilera, pp. 20–21.

Bogotá (Civil Engineering and Military School of Bogotá). He graduated with distinction in three years, instead of five. While studying there, he also taught Spanish, algebra, geometry and trigonometry.

When he returned to Panama, he worked for the *Compagnie Universelle du Canal Inter-Oceanique* in 1888. The same year, Abel Bravo endeavoured together with other Panamanians to design a law for the foundation of a secondary school in Panama (Law 83 of 1888). The Colegio Balboa was established in 1889 and became the only institution of public secondary education or *Liceo* (Lyceum) in Panama. Bravo was named its first rector. He stayed in that position until 1892. Finally, in 1895, he was named Secretary of Public Instruction of the Department of Panama by Governor Ricardo Arango. Not long after, he was also in charge of the Secretary of the Government and of Finances. Hence, he was taking care of all the Secretariats between 1895 and 1896. He resigned due to health issues and then travelled to Costa Rica, Canada, the United States and Europe.[86] While travelling and just after his return, the Government of Colombia delegated upon him some of the most important tasks in delimitating the frontiers with Costa Rica and Venezuela. After the Independence of Panama, he briefly occupied the position of Secretary of Public Instruction. In 1907, as a representative at the National Assembly, he designed the law for the creation of the Instituto Nacional (founded in 1909),[87] which would become the most important school in the Isthmus in the twentieth century.

On 24 April 1890, Bravo commented on the Colegio Balboa and on the general situation of education in Panama. This text was included in the bi-annual report of the Minister of Public Instruction of Colombia on 1890. There Bravo celebrated the 'patriotic' effort of the Colombian government to promote public instruction in Panama. He claimed that without its help, the Colegio Balboa would not have opened so soon. However, he was critical of the conditions of schooling in Panama, including: the lack of teaching materials, school tools, texts and a suitable building. Just as pernicious for him though, was the 'general indifference for instruction' in the Isthmus.[88] He added that:

---

[86] Ibid., p. 20.
[87] Sociedad Geográfica de Colombia, p. 5.
[88] Bravo, p. 292.

Because Panamanian education is in its infancy, it is not possible, at the moment for the [Colegio Balboa] to function at full capacity; there are not enough students with the capacities that would allow them to study at the Lyceum level ... [Therefore] the Colegio Balboa forcefully demands that teaching appeals to the lowest common denominator, because of the lamentable intellectual backwardness in which Panamanian youth finds itself.[89]

Therefore, he opted for founding a preparatory school with a 'permanent character', so that the students could enrol there first and obtain the necessary knowledge to reach secondary school level.[90] He also decided to refound and incorporate a primary school for the boys of San Felipe (the central and walled neighbourhood of the colonial city), which had not existed 'in a long time', as part of the whole system. The plan was that after finishing primary school level, the students would go into the preparatory school, and later upgrade and move into the Lyceum.[91] The Colegio Balboa system started with ninety-two students, 'all of them in a shameful state of ignorance', emphasized Bravo.[92]

By 1 July 1889, the students of the Colegio Balboa and the annexed primary school were being classified and divided in groups. At that instance, there were fifty-six students in primary school, forty-four in preparatory school, and thirty-five in the Lyceum.[93] Despite the fact that enrolment for the second year of the Colegio Balboa and its associated schools was supposed to end on 31 March 1890, it was necessary to expand it to 30 April 1890 to increase the quantity of students. There was an explanation: 'many families were absent from [Panama City] as they had left for summer vacations'.[94] As a result, the number of students increased from 135 to 178; there were 140 students in the primary school, but only nineteen in both the preparatory and Lyceum (a total of thirty-eight).[95] Bravo seemed sympathetic with the so-called '*estudiantes internados*' (boarding students) from the countryside. He understood that

[89] Ibid., pp. 292–293.
[90] Ibid., p. 292.
[91] Ibid., p. 293.
[92] Ibid.
[93] Ibid.
[94] Ibid., p. 294.
[95] Ibid.

they might begin classes late, in June or July, due to the parents' lack of finances for provisioning their children with uniform and school materials.[96] Other issues included the locations of the Colegio Balboa. Bravo, as a civil engineer, was aware of the contemporary issues of proper housing, urbanism and health, and how these impacted schooling. When describing the conditions of the Colegio Balboa building, he wrote that:

> Besides being small and located in a dark and narrow street, it occupies a central place in town, where the noise of vehicles constantly interrupts teaching. The patio is not very spacious for the primary school students to do their gymnastic exercises … There is not a single bath or latrine for the employees [i.e., the directors and teachers] and the private ones for the students barely amount to 4 … The building known as … *Las Monjas* [The Nuns] is the best and perhaps the only one that can work for hosting the Colegio [de Balboa] … it is close to the sea, where there are no [nearby] houses, which makes it well-lit, cool, quiet and healthy; it has beautiful gardens and alleys, a fresh water cistern.[97]

As the name suggests, the building of *Las Monjas* was a colonial convent, but later became a prison and military barracks. That is, aside from providing a healthy and non-noise polluted environment for students and teachers, its design was that of a panopticon, where students (or nuns, prisoners and soldiers) could be observed from every angle to keep the school's discipline and guarantee proper learning.

In relation to actual teaching, Bravo mentioned that the admission process followed those indicated by the Organic Law of 1887, which indicated that secondary schools in Colombia should adopt the entrance requirement of the Colegio del Rosario in Bogotá, the main higher education institution of the country.[98] Despite this, Bravo still indicated that the performance of students was 'satisfactory'.[99] Contrary to other intellectuals and pedagogues in Latin America of the period,[100] Bravo was not pessimistic or derogatory in a racial manner. His account might show disappointment, but he did not condemn the students and did not doubt the possibility of overcoming 'ignorance' or 'intellectual backwardness'.

[96] Ibid.
[97] Ibid., p. 296.
[98] Ibid., p. 295.
[99] Ibid., p. 294.
[100] Again see, Michela Coletta. *Decadent Modernity. Civilization and 'Latinidad' in Spanish America 1880–1920*. (Liverpool: Liverpool University Press, 2018).

Most of his report approved the policies of *La Regeneración*. Bravo concluded his report by asserting that 'the inauguration of this schooling establishment means the beginning of an epoch of scientific regeneration for the Department of Panama'.[101] Bravo also details his solutions and his hyperbolic narrative of crisis becomes a story of salvation.

His speech is an example of the exaltation of the 'ideal of the practical' as most of his exposition used a technocratic language that focused on numerical and practical information: number of students, lists of books and courses, names of teachers, salaries, and a description of the building. Problems could be measured or detailed empirically, and solutions could be found in a pragmatic manner.

The Catholic Language and Imagery of the Panamanian Pedagogical Elite: Melchor Lasso de la Vega
Before entering the pedagogical elite, Lasso de la Vega had directed the public schools of towns and capitals of the countryside at Pocrí, his hometown Aguadulce and Santiago. Later, he became Inspector of Public Instruction of the Provinces of Coclé and Veraguas. He also was one of the directors of the Colegio del Istmo, a short-lived private All-Men Secondary School. In 1897, he was already Sub-Secretary of Public Instruction of the Department of Panama. In addition, he travelled to Costa Rica, where he directed some schools. By 1906, he was the Secretary of Public Instruction of the Republic of Panama.[102]

In 1897, *Reseña Escolar* published speeches in honour of a deceased teacher, Eugenio Vásquez. There was an obituary by José de la Rosa Poveda, a graduate from the *Escuela Normal de Varones*, which compared Vásquez to an apostle and his qualities of good teacher, good father and good citizen to a sort of 'Holy Trinity' that 'irradiated goodness'.[103] Yet the most philosophical speech was presented by Mélchor Lasso de la Vega. He compared the deceased teacher to a soldier. He mourned

---

[101] Bravo, p. 296.

[102] Aguilera. *Galería de Hombres Públicos* ..., pp. 44–45.

[103] José De la Rosa Poveda. 'Discursos pronunciados ante el cadáver del Señor Eugenio Vásquez, Director de la sección media de la escuela de varones de Calidonia. Discurso por el Señor José de la Rosa Poveda, Director de la sección elemental número 2 de la Escuela de Varones de San Felipe, Comisionado de la Secretaría de I. Pública y por el cuerpo de maestros de la capital' in *Reseña Escolar. Periódico Oficial de Instrucción Pública*. Tomo V. N° 54, Panamá: Imprenta de Pacífico Vega, 16 de Octubre de 1897, pp. 2–3.

Vásquez's sudden death with the following phrase: 'surprised by death in the toughest moment of combat was the only way he could abandon the battlefield'.[104] Nonetheless, this comparison contrasted a time in which 'the noise of weapons thundered everywhere' and the victors 'enslaved' the defeated with a new era in which the heroes attempted to dissipate 'shadows' and free spirits.[105] The former period seems a reference to the times prior to *La Regeneración*; the latter appears as a time of peaceful struggle in favour of progress and of education. Hence, in spite of the references to wars and weapons, Lasso de la Vega's message, rather than transmitting a valorisation of military glory, granted more merit to the Vásquez's career as an educator and holder of Christian values. This can be noticed when Lasso de la Vega described him as a person who did not involve himself in politics, nor dreamt of the 'triumphs reaped in the fields of destruction'.[106] Lasso de la Vega celebrated the idea that Vásquez was a good Christian, who became involved in the most humble, fruitful and crucial of careers: teaching.[107] For him, Vasquez helped to open up space to the 'priests of science' and to a 'soldier' that fought only with 'faith' against ignorance.[108] Lasso de la Vega's metaphor was not a call to arms; instead, it was a modelling of a non-military hero. Rather than imitating a reactionary Catholic discourse, his speech comprised concepts closely related to what Rafael Núñez defined as *Paz Científica*. Even though some similarities are observable between the discourses of José Telésforo Paúl and Lasso de la Vega, the latter's words were less aggressive. Moral regeneration and Christian education appear as crucial, but the rhetoric against liberalism and science was not necessarily the epicentre of Lasso de la Vega's speech.

[104] Melchor Lasso de la Vega. 'Discursos pronunciados ante el cadáver del Señor Eugenio Vásquez, Director de la sección media de la escuela de varones de Calidonia. Discurso del Señor M. Lasso de la Vega. Oficial Mayor de Instrucción Pública. *Reseña Escolar*, Tomo V. N° 54. Panamá: 16 de octubre de 1897, p. 4.

[105] Ibid.

[106] Ibid., p. 3.

[107] Ibid.

[108] Ibid., p. 4.

PART III. *LA REGENERACIÓN* IN SCHOOLS

A study of the curricula and list of courses, the members of the faculty, a list of books and the assessment helps to better comprehend to what extent the political reform, its language and its expectations were injected into the educational system, particularly into Isthmian schools. It also serves to understand to what point teachers and students interiorized them, whether as transmitting agents or as receptors. Nevertheless, it is relevant to recognise that without sources that explicitly illustrate the students' perspectives, the panorama is still incomplete. Although there is little information about students' opinions and absorption of teachings, and about what happened daily in classrooms and schools, it is possible to get hints through the list of courses, reports on performances and grades, information about who taught a class or assessed the students, and the analysis of books used for each course.

El Colegio Balboa

As mentioned, the Colegio Balboa was the first secondary school founded in Panama after the consolidation of *La Regeneración* in 1886. Bravo's report of 1890 offers useful insights about how *La Regeneración* was taken into that secondary school.

Curricula

Whilst not all those involved in the education system taught with the intent of exploiting their pupils, in Colombian Panama the idea of implanting a particular view of 'proper' nationalism was not only relevant for instilling obedience, but also for mobilising citizens towards order, progress and modernity. The search for 'constant perfectioning' through positive co-existence and cooperation was perceived as a progressive means to modernity.[109] However, it was pre-empted that students could reject the values of the education system by being influenced by other agents like their parents, friends, priests, neighbours, politicians and even 'corrupt teachers'. Examples of this defiance could be missing classes, refusing to study, bad behaviour, cheating, contesting or questioning the teacher's knowledge and authority. Fears and hopes, projects of abjection, and the

---

[109] Reinhart Kosselleck. *Futures Past. On the Semantics of Historical Time.* Keith Tribe, trans. (New York: Columbia University Press, 2004), pp. 265–266. Also Thomas S. Popkewitz,. *Cosmopolitanism and the Age of School Reform. Science, Education, and the Making of the Child.* (New York: Routledge, 2008). p. 17.

search for a particular kind of progress do not necessarily mean that there
is an intent to use education and 'the hidden curriculum' to force a pre-
designed structure on young minds.[110] Pereyra, Popkewitz and Franklin
explain that education is more about persuasion than coercion to attain
authority.[111] So, the curriculum was constantly reformed to reach or find
the track towards perfecting individuals and society. The supposed aim of
the Colegio de Balboa's conservative and nationalist curriculum was to
help regenerate the country by domesticating students' agency in a seemingly benign manner.

In 1890, Bravo's report provided a list of courses, teachers and books
used at the Colegio Balboa (see Annex 3). Regarding the curricula, the
Colegio Balboa had courses in arithmetic (Levels I and II), Castilian grammar (i.e., Spanish grammar), universal and Colombian geography, religion
(Levels I and II), calligraphy, historia patria (fatherland history), sacred
history, Latin and 'ideological reading and composition'.[112] Although it is
not mentioned in the study programme, the list of books includes another
course on urban themes.[113]

There is no description of the content of the courses or the hours dedicated to them, but it is possible to infer that there was a considerable
emphasis on knowledge regarding the Colombian nation. However, the
list of courses seems to give more importance to morality and national
religion. Besides three courses explicitly on religion (Course I and II and
sacred history), there was a fourth on proper moral and social behaviour
(urbanity). There was a strong emphasis on Spanish, the national language: a course in Spanish grammar and another on calligraphy. It is not
clear what was the content of the course of 'ideological reading and composition', but the name suggests that it was related to the adequate use of
language and possibly religion or conservatism. One course represented a
combination of technical or practical knowledge with that of the characteristics of the nation: geography of Colombia. This was complemented
with a course that taught about the rest of the world, an important element for a country who wanted to be part of 'modern civilisation', looked
for inspiration in models from Europe and the United States, and wanted

---

[110] Franklin, Pereyra and Popkewitz, pp. 10–11.

[111] Ibid. For more on the notion of persuasion and authority, look at Barrington Moore Jr.
Injustice. The Social Basis of Obedience and Revolt. (New York: M. E. Sharpe Inc., 1978),
pp. 17–23 and 440–445.

[112] Bravo ..., p. 295.

[113] Ibid., p. 293.

to attract investment and cultural exchange. There was a class on national history. The study of Latin symbolised both an attachment to the Church as well as to Roman (occidental) civilisation.[114] Finally, there was only one course purely focused in technical and practical aspects: arithmetic. Similarly, the students of the Preparatory School learned about geography, reading, calligraphy, religion, sacred history, arithmetic and Castilian grammar.[115] The focus was placed again on knowledge about the Colombia nation,[116] as there were two courses in Spanish, as well as in religion. There were also two technical courses: geography and arithmetic.

Teachers

Equally important is to look at the teachers who facilitated the classes in both the Lyceum and the Preparatory School. This is important in order to recognise the networks and social spaces of the pedagogical elite and students, but also to notice the relations of intellectual authority between teacher and students. That is, it sheds light upon the kind of image that persons who taught and tamed students had as role models for future citizens. At the Lyceum, Abel Bravo himself was the teacher of arithmetic, Spanish grammar and 'ideological reading and composition'. Since he was an engineer and with his experience at the Escuela de Ingeniería Civil y Militar de Bogotá, he was prepared to teach these courses. Of no less importance is the fact that the teacher of religion Levels I and II, sacred history and Latin was a Jesuit priest, Presbítero Javier Junguito (1843–1911), who would be Bishop of Panama from 1901 to 1911. At the preparatory level, Manuel Valentín Bravo taught geography, reading and calligraphy, while another priest, Eugenio Navarro, gave lessons on religion and sacred history. In summary, the highest authority of the Colegio and his brother defined the content and teaching methods of most of the topics related to the national language and technical knowledge, while two priests, mainly Javier Junguito, taught the material for the inculcation of moral and religious values. The relevance of religion, though, comes to light when Bravo reported that students 'complied'

---

[114] For similar examples in Latin America see: Andrew Laird and Nicola Miller, eds. *Antiquities and Classical Traditions in Latin America.* (London: Wiley, 2018).

[115] Bravo, p. 295.

[116] Nicola Miller. Keynote Speaker. 'Republics of Knowledge in Latin America' in *I Congreso de Historia, Antropología y Turismo Histórico-Cultural,* (Panamá: Universidad de Panamá, 2019).

with their religious duties, because they 'confessed and received the Eucharist'.[117] He added that making students comply with religious study was of extreme importance because this enhanced the practice of Catholicism, which was 'generally uncared for by the youth of Colombia'.[118]

Books
The government of Colombia wrote and approved the curricula and the textbooks used in schools. Hence, the curricula selected specific textbooks to teach religion, urbanity, fatherland history, Colombian geography and Spanish. These show how the local authorities reinforced the discourse and process of nation-building of *La Regeneración* in Isthmian schools.

Bravo's report mentioned that the students were to use the following reading materials: arithmetic by Lavalle; *Ortología y Analogía* (Orthoepy and Analogy) and by Roa; *Compendio de Geografía de Colombia* and *Compendio de Geografía Universal* (Compendium of Geography of Colombia and Compendium of Universal Geography) by politician and intellectual Carlos Martínez Silva; *Manual de urbanidad y buenas maneras* by Venezuelan Manuel Antonio Carreño; and a book on religion by F. H. Schouppe and *Exposición Demostrada de la Doctrina Cristiana* (Demonstrated Exposition of Christian Doctrine) by Colombian textbook writer Juan B. Ortíz.[119] Bravo pointed out that there were some books missing, though, so 'it was necessary to use the [books] that were sold in [Panama] City, even if they were not the official ones, as it happened with the ones on Geography and Latin, because if not, it would have not been possible to start classes'.[120] In addition, many students, however, lacked books, since the textbooks for religion (Schouppe and Ortíz) and *Historia Patria* (Fatherland's History) had not yet arrived in Panama. Reacting to the de-acceleration towards progress, Bravo indicated that 'the lack of books hinders the advancement of the students'.[121] Nevertheless, the fact that he opted to buy and use books that were not included in the curricula to begin the school year indicates that local educational authorities, such as the directors, general inspector or Secretaries of Public Instruction of

[117] Bravo, p. 294.
[118] Ibid.
[119] Ibid., p. 293.
[120] Ibid.
[121] Ibid., p. 294.

Panama, as well as school directors, had a margin of action for problem-solving related to limited resources and other unexpected events that posed obstacles to national policies.

Grades

Summative assessments through exams show, more than anything, the perspective of the teachers, inspectors and educational authorities regarding what should be assessed and how rigorously it should be evaluated. Both of these aspects of evaluation respond to the examiners' subjectivity, an impediment to effectively understand the reasons why students performed well or poorly in a particular topic or in general. There are many possibilities: the examiners were too indulgent or too strict; the student did not study adequately; the lessons in the classrooms were stimulating or not; or, perhaps there were animosities and scepticism from the evaluators towards a student or group of students. Nevertheless, grades do show that, at least, some students tried to pass and that those who did well fulfilled the examiners expectations, possibly attracting their interest and support. Nevertheless, Bravo's report of 1890 mentioned that the students of the Colegio Balboa took constant 'Prácticas Sabatinas' (roughly Sabbatical Exams) 'to know the state of the classes, correct flaws in teaching ... [and] introduce all the necessary modifications'.[122] For him, the exams not only had the purpose of imposing a message on students; they gave teachers the opportunity to learn and adjust their teaching methodology. He did not provide the results of these tests in 1890, though.

In 1897, however, *Reseña Escolar* did publish the results of the trimestral 'Sabatino' Exams (See Annex 4).[123] The number of topics evaluated show that the curricula had been changed considerably. By then, the students of Colegio Balboa took Castilian I and Castilian II (i.e., Spanish I and II); arithmetic I and II; descriptive geography; English I and II; French I and II; Latin I and II; religion I and II; historia patria (fatherland history); algebra; philosophy; and accounting. The number of technical topics had increased to include accounting and add one more level of arithmetic. A course on descriptive geography replaced those of Colombian and universal geographies. Philosophy, French, English and another level

---

[122] Ibid.

[123] Esteban Terradas 'Acta de los exámenes denominados "sabatina" verificados en día 1ro y 2do del presente mes de octubre', *Reseña Escolar* Tomo V. No. 54, Panama: 16 de octubre de 1897, pp. 824–825.

of Latin were incorporated to sum up together with fatherland history and Spanish six more classes on the humanities. The emphasis on national and moral knowledge seemed to dilute by the end of the nineteenth century, because the curricula transformed into a more cosmopolitan and practical instrument. But this might be just an illusion, since the Father of Calasanz ruled the Colegio Balboa and monitored the content of the courses and exams. Language and philosophy, as well as technical courses such as descriptive geography and accounting might instil morally mediated visions of the present future by religious visions of nature or teaching honesty in accountancy from a conservative perspective. On the day of the sabbatical exams, several students were assessed. They barely passed arithmetic I and II, religion I, and Latin I with a grade of 3. However, their performance in the rest was acceptable to excellent obtaining grades between 4 and 5. The fact that there was an improvement in religion and Latin suggests that the students were showing progress in the eyes of their teachers and the priests. Still, how much of this knowledge was interiorised and used through their personal life and careers is a mystery so far.

The Escuela Normal de Institutoras: *Students, Curricula and Grades*

In 1897, *Reseña Escolar* published the list of names, the title of courses, and the grades of the students of the *Escuela Normal de Institutoras*. The school had thirty-three students (see Annex 5). An interesting fact is that some of the students had the same surname as that of the graduates from the *Escuela Normal de Varones* from the 1870s and 1880s or of the contemporary authorities. It is possible then to suggest a family connection, which might imply that teaching was seen as a family trade for certain middle sectors of Panamanian society.

The *Escuela Normal de Institutoras* had a somewhat different curricula to the one of the Colegio Balboa, but the purposes were similar: taming the future teacher as a route to reproduce the domestication of coming generations of children; provide the graduates with technical and moral knowledge to ensure progress according to the prerogatives of the conservative-positivist government; create a 'space of experience' for current and future teachers, where the *Escuela Normal de Institutoras* represents the most crucial moment in the forging of their professional and ideological identities; and to give them a 'horizon of expectations' related to an economically stable future, the potential to remain in the same social spaces or even enter new one, through the acquisition of a new cultural capital.

Out of all the knowledge that they would acquire, the one in pedagogics was a symbol of specialisation and uniqueness that could open a door to a better economic, political or social status. The other courses were: reading, writing, Spanish, arithmetic, geometry, religion, sacred history, calisthenics, geography of Colombia, physical geography, urbanity and drawing.[124] Again, the information does not indicate how many hours were dedicated to each topic and very little is said about course content and class material. Nevertheless, the emphasis on national culture and technical topics is noticeable in the list of courses. On the one hand there were the topics focusing on national culture and related to conservative notions of morality: writing, reading, Spanish, religion and sacred history. On the other, there were the technical courses: physical geography, arithmetic, geometry, calisthenics and drawing. There were those courses that mixed both areas, such as the geography of Colombia.

In the report of the Secretary of Public Instruction of the Department of Panama of 1898, there is an interesting comment that some of the *teachers of the Escuela Normal de Institutoras* were members of the pedagogical elite: Melchor Lasso de la Vega taught Spanish grammar, geometry (applied to drawing) and arithmetic, and Salomón Ponce Aguilera took care of the classes on religion and sacred history. Also, German pedagogue Max Lemm facilitated the courses on drawing and calisthenics. Of importance is that the curricula addressed the Colombian and Panamanian society views on the role of women. In October 1897, a class in music and singing was added. The teacher hired for the class was the future composer of Panama's national anthem, Spaniard Santos Jorge.[125] So, the students of the *Escuela Normal de Institutoras* had classes with key members of the pedagogical elite and professionals and pedagogues from abroad.

There were many motivations for incorporating the course on singing. According to law, this course was necessary for the 'education of the noble sentiments of the child'. The reason why it had not been included in elementary schools was the lack of expertise of existing teachers. Hence, the

---

[124] Based on: Matilde Rubiano C. and Rosa H. Rubiano C. *Escuela Normal de Institutoras.* Registro Correspondiente al Mes de Septiembre, *Reseña Escolar* Tomo V. No. 54, Panamá: 16 de octubre de 1897, pp. 822–823. Matilde Rubiano C. and Rosa H. Rubiano C. *Escuela Normal de Institutoras.* Registro Correspondiente al Mes de Octubre, *Reseña Escolar.* Tomo V. No. 55, Panamá: 15 de noviembre de 1897, pp. 837–838. Matilde Rubiano C. and Rosa H. Rubiano C. *Escuela Normal de Institutoras.* Registro Correspondiente al Mes de Noviembre, *Reseña Escolar* Tomo V. No. 56, Panamá: 15 de diciembre de 1897, pp. 849–850.

[125] Secretaría de Instrucción Pública del Departamento de Panamá. 'Decreto No. 47 del 30 de septiembre 1897', *Reseña Escolar* Tomo V. No. 54, Panamá: 16 de octubre de 1897, p. 821.

educational authorities decided to provide the future female teachers with musical skills. Nevertheless, another reason was surely the social views of the era that construed knowledge about art and music as conducive to a well-mannered and educated woman. This was especially important for those who were asked to teach morality and manners by example and wanted to use their career as teachers to socially mobilise. In addition, singing was also important for the Church, as many ceremonies and the mass required singing and choirs. In sum, the course on music and singing was a matter of teaching through performability and repetition as a way for instilling certain desired values and behaviours in female teachers.

The tables presented in *Reseña Escolar* showed that each student was assessed according to three values: attendance, 'lesson' and conduct. It does not seem that these values affected each other in calculating the final summative grade, but the subjectivity of teachers might have. Attendance was registered, but the sources suggest that only a few students tended to constantly miss classes. 'Lesson' referred to the actual academic performance of the student and was likely evaluated applying exams, classwork and/or homework. The exception was the course in urbanity, which did not have a register for attendance or receive a grading for 'lesson'. The reason for this could be that there were no classes and exams, and/or the evaluation was done by observing the conduct of each single student at the school. Surprisingly, this course did not receive any evaluation in the month of November 1897.

The fact that the grades were published in a periodical represents an act of coercion. Whether *Reseña Escolar* was widely read or not, there was always a chance that other students' parents, teachers, classmates, ecclesiastical and political authorities could see the grades. A poorly performing student could be socially exposed and ridiculed. This possibly the case of students who got terrible grades in urbanity, for they could seen unclean, poorly-mannered, and uncivilised. Similarly, when calculating the final grades or 'Liquidación' (Liquidation), the school's teachers and authorities, including Colombian director Matilde Rubiano C. and sub-director Rosa H. Rubiano C., rounded the grade down. It illustrates that their posture on assessment was severely strict. Almost reaching a high grade was not enough, and it should not be rewarded but punished. After calculating the average of all grades per course, I was able to see that the students of the *Escuela Normal de Institutoras* performed better in calisthenics (4,78); sacred history (4,70); drawing (4,65); and religion (4,59). However, their achievements in music and singing (4,15), physical geography (4,05), arithmetic (3,84) and writing (3,71) were not the most satisfactory, especially considering that their grade would be reduced to the closest and lowest single natural number. Nevertheless, after estimating the overall average of all the grades obtained in September, October and November 1897, it was possible to see that only one student did not get passing grades, but there were many who got perfect grades (5). This suggests that there was a high graduation rate. Unfortunately, they could not study when the War of the Thousand Days began in 1899.

Education in the Countryside: Parental Indifference and Provision of Practical but Limited Knowledge

El Precursor of Santiago de Veraguas was a newspaper published by conservative Ladislao Sosa, a musician and former elementary school student of Nicolás Victoria Jaén.[126] In 1896, this periodical released an article with the title of 'La Instrucción Pública', which argued that public instruction required reform and that social conditions should determine the kind of education a child should receive. Poor parents made a considerable effort to send their children to school thinking they would obtain 'useful knowledge for real life', instead of ornamental knowledge such as grammar, history and geography. The article proposed that rural instruction should concentrate on basic writing and reading, arithmetic and Christian doctrine.[127] These were counterintuitive notions of pedagogics and advancement: the proposed plan suggested that limiting the provision of knowledge to the mere basic for poor rural children would generate more material and spiritual benefits in relatively isolated countryside areas, where people depended on their family's farming activities to subsist. The proposal also constrained children to duplicate their parents' style of living. This proposal was surely beneficial for landowners who depended on hand labour on their estates.

Most inspectors of public instruction and practicing teachers in the countryside seem to disagree, as they evaluated all aspects of the curriculum. This can be observed in the reports that the Inspectors of Public Instruction of different provinces wrote after they visited and assessed schools in small towns.[128] For instance, in 1897, Jacinto Ponce, former

---

[126] Rodolfo Aguilera. *Galería de Hombres Públicos del Istmo*. (Panamá: Tipografía de Casis y Cia, 1906), pp. 61–62.

[127] *El Precursor: Periódico de intereses generales*. Año I, N° 4. Santiago de Veraguas, Panamá: Imprenta y Encuadernación de Ladislao Sosa, Julio 15 de 1896, p. 2.

[128] To see other meticulous reports: 'Lorenzo Barraza. Informe No. 10. República de Colombia—Departamento de Panamá—Inspección de Instrucción Pública de la Provincia de Chiriquí—David, Febrero 12 de 1897', *Reseña Escolar: Periódico oficial de Instrucción*

student of the *Escuela Normal de Varones* wrote detailed reports about the situation of schools in the Province of Coclé. His visits consisted of interviewing the school's teacher or director; analysing the teaching techniques; the condition of books; counting the number of students that attended that day versus the enrolled students; observing the students' behaviour; teaching a 'model course' probably to provide an example on proper teaching; testing the children in two to four topics; and noting their compliance with religious duties. These were, after all, the minimum requirements that the discourse of *La Regeneración* proposed for initiating the moral rejuvenation and material progress of the poor.[129]

As can be seen in Table 3.1 on the evaluation of attendance and academic and religious performance, Ponce provide interesting comments about excelling schools like the All-Men School of Antón, especially of great students like José de J. Rangel, who performed highly in all topics. Ponce highlighted that Rangel was particularly good at poetry and prose. In addition, he congratulated his former schoolmate, Benigno Andrión for elevating the display of knowledge in all levels of the All-Men School of Penonomé. He also explained that in some schools, the low attendance was due to illness and the need for students to help parents in agricultural activities or because it was too distant as happened with the All-Girls Schools of La Pintada and the mixed-School of Río Grande. The emphasis in the assessment was placed on the tests on the aforementioned 'practical knowledges' (reading, writing, grammar, arithmetic), as well as religion and sacred history. Sometimes, the students were tested on national knowledge by not only evaluating their level of Spanish and religion, but also of fatherland history.

It seems that there was no clear prejudice about the topics that female and male students should take. However, Ponce did write an observation asking for higher levels of education for the All-Girls School of Penonomé:

> It is a delicate matter that the scarcity of qualified teachers deprives the youth of such a beautiful gender that grows in Penonomé of the benefits of public instruction, [thus] frustrating the efforts and sacrifices of the government. Hopefully, to alleviate this evil and to satisfy the just aspirations of the

Pública. Tomo V. No. 48 Panamá: Imprenta de Pacífico Vega, 10 de abril de 1897, pp. 719–722.

[129] Jacinto Ponce. 'Informe Número 2. República de Colombia—Departamento de Panamá—Dirección de Instrucción Pública de la Provincia del Coclé—Antón—Agosto 18 de 1897' in Ibid., pp. 826–828.

Table 3.1 Report on inspections at school of the province of Coclé by Jacinto Ponce in August 1897

School	Director/Teacher	Students Evaluated/Enrolled	Behaviour	Tests	Result	Religious Duties
All-Girl Anton	Leonor A. Quintero	30/46	Very Good	Reading Grammar Religion	Pass Pass Pass	Compliance
All-Men Anton	José A. Casís	57/77—Student José de J. Rangel exalted for his performance	Very Good	Reading Grammar Arithmetic Fatherland History	Very Good Very Good Very Good Very Good	N.A.
All-Men Penonome (Elementary and Middle)	Benigno Andrión (*Escuela Normal de Varones* Graduate) - Praised for his achievements.	72/104	Good	Reading Arithmetic Sacred History Religion	Very Good Very Good Very Good	Compliance
All-Girls Penenome (Elementary)	Inés Herrera	60/73	Good	Reading Arithmetic Sacred History	Very Good Some Progress—Pass Pass Pass	Compliance

(continued)

Table 3.1 (continued)

School	Director/Teacher	Students Evaluated/Enrolled	Behaviour	Tests	Result	Religious Duties
All-Men La Pintada	Isaac Fernández V.	16/25	Good	Grammar Fatherland History Sacred History	Very Satisfied Very Satisfied Very Satisfied	No Compliance (No Priest)
All-Girls La Pintada	Teacher did not Attend	Lack of Attendance: only 6 (No Inspection)	No Inspection	No Inspection	No Inspection	No Inspection
Mixed Río Grande	Belermina Ocaña	18	Good	Reading Drawing Religion Arithmetic	Satisfied Satisfied Satisfied Satisfied	No Compliance (No Priest)
All-Men Natá	Vianor Apolayo (*Escuela Normal de Varones* Graduate).	18 / 33	Poor—Students disrespected the teacher and the Inspector	N.A.	N.A.	Compliance

Source: see the reports published in *Reseña Escolar: Periódico oficial de Instrucción Pública.* Tomo V, N° 48, 50, 54–56. Panamá: Imprenta de Pacífico Vega, 10 de Abril de 1897–15 de Diciembre de 1897

Panamanian society ... an intern would be hired that could be in charge of the sections related to middle and secondary school.[130]

Hardly a complete campaign for gender equality, Ponce seemed to understand the need for promoting women's education in the countryside and the Isthmus in general.

CONCLUSION: THE PERMANENCE OF *LA REGENERACIÓN* IN PANAMANIAN EDUCATION AFTER 1903

This chapter studied the connections of scientists, the Catholic Church, and educators with the governments of Colombia and Panama. This unveiled more than ties of political and ideological affinity and discursive similarities; it discovered a consensus about the necessity of moral rejuvenation and the shared intent to the pursuit of 'technocratic modernity' to bring about progress. This helped to explain why Conservative professionals with technical or scientific careers, such as Ricardo Arango and Manuel Amador Guerrero, named educators Pacheco, Bravo, Victoria Jaen and Lasso de la Vega as authorities within the educational system of Panama after 1903.

Loaded with positive expectations, these educators imagined a nation that had progressed through a process of moral rejuvenation and purification, as well as the proper application of knowledge. The fact that the members of the pedagogical elite remained in high positions within the Secretariat of Public Instruction and the educational system after 1903 suggests that they kept reproducing and divulging the ideas of *La Regeneración* in periodicals and speeches. An example of this is Nicolás Victoria Jaén's article 'Los niños, según el evangelio' (Children, according to the gospel) published in *Reseña Escolar* in 1908.[131] The text analysed two passages of the Bible in which Jesus Christ talked about children and the Kingdom of Heaven.[132] According to Victoria Jaén, these verses

---

[130] Ibid., p. 827.

[131] The editor, actually, added a note indicating that the article was taken from 'El lector istmeño' in *Reseña Escolar*, Ano° 4 N° 4. Panamá: Secretaría de Instrucción Pública, 4 de abril de 1908, p. 88.

[132] Specifically, the author referred to *The Gospel of Matthew*. Chapter XVIII. Victoria Jaén. 'Los niños, según el evangelio' in *Reseña Escolar*. Ano° 4 N° 4. Panamá: Secretaría de Instrucción Pública, 4 de abril de 1908, p. 88.

showed that Christ had a preference for children due to their humility, innocence and 'blind and practical faith'.[133] Jesus protected them, because, as mankind is selfish, many children were left without education and physical nurture. The 'Divine Master', said Victoria Jaén, wants to 'teach'[134] humanity that He cared about children, and, more importantly, that He would compensate those who take care of them and teach them. Next, this Panamanian educator focused on the punishment that Jesus assigned to those who 'offended' children. If offending children was punishable, then teaching with the intention of corrupting them deserved a worse chastisement.[135] According to Victoria Jaén's text, children have a natural tendency towards good deeds.[136] Hence, the worse form of corruption was to teach children that God did not exist and to act against the 'divine precepts', because this would 'kill' the children's faith.[137] Ultimately, Victoria Jaén argued that, when Jesus 'suggested' his disciples to take care of young people, he was placing children under the protection of the Church.[138]

Although simple, the writing seems to be a metaphoric call to educators to behave within Christian precepts and to serve as models to children. By promising a divine reward, Victoria Jaén was not only promoting Christian values, but also recruiting new teachers with strong Catholic values. At the same time, he was discouraging non-religious or atheist teachers from even considering a teaching career. This is reminiscent of the passages written by the Bishop of Panama, José Telésforo Paúl, in his letters to his parish of 1876 and 1883, when he also discouraged non-Catholic educators. The author's analysis of the Bible explicitly showed his support for religious teaching and a justification for the Church in children's education. In the same context, these were necessary to avoid the moral corruption of children and, therefore, of society. In addition, it brings back the arguments of the Bishop, Casas Rojas and Bravo: teachers' have to imitate Jesus and see the children's innocence and 'natural tendency' to behave well as a symbol of an empty mind and soul that needs intellectual,

[133] Ibid.
[134] It is possible that Victoria Jaén was playing when using the word 'Maestro'. The word in this context seems to have a double connotation as both 'master' and 'teacher'. Depending on the connotation, 'enseñarle' would acquire a slightly different meaning.
[135] Ibid., p. 90.
[136] Ibid.
[137] Ibid.
[138] Ibid.

moral and spiritual guidance. Properly taught using the Gospel, they will keep their 'blinded and practical' faith and become productive and harmless adults. Nevertheless, if students were corrupted by teaching them atheist or sinful ideas, they would damage society in the present and future. The teachers who did this should be punished for endangering society. The article represents both hope and 'double gestures' applied to educators and youth. In short, it preserved many elements of conservative and Catholic views of progress and modernity.

BIBLIOGRAPHY

Aguilera, Rodolfo. *Galería de Hombres Públicos del Istmo.* (Panamá: Tipografía de Casis y Cia, 1906).

Baldomedo Carles V. *Informe del Rector del Seminario de Panamá. Rectorado del Seminario – Sección 9ᵃ – Numero 4, Informe que el Ministro de Instrucción Pública presenta al Congreso de Colombia en sus sesiones de 1890.* (Bogotá: Imprenta de 'La Luz, 3 de julio de 1890).

Bernal, Juan Bosco. 'La Educación en Panamá: antecedentes, tendencias y perspectivas'. *Panamá: Cien Años de República.* (Panamá: Comisión Universitaria del Centenario de la República, 2004).

Biografías Panameñas. Biblioteca Nacional de Panamá. www.binal.ac.pa.

Bushnell, David. *The Making of Modern Colombia. A nation in spite of itself* (Berkeley, Los Angeles, London: University of California Press, 1993).

Cantón, Alfredo. *Desenvolvimiento de las Ideas Pedagógicas en Panamá 1903–1926.* (Panamá: Imprenta Nacional, 1955).

Casas Rojas, Jesús. *Informe Presentado al Congreso de Colombia en su Sesión de 1888.* (Bogotá: Unclear Publisher, n.d.).

Cedeño Cenci, Diógenes (?) Sociedad de Geográfica de Colombia and Academia de Ciencias Geográficas. 'Rasgos Biográficos de Don Abel Bravo (1861–1934)' in Artículo del Boletín de la Sociedad de Geográfica de Colombia. No 77-78. Vol. XXI (Bogotá: Sociedad de Geográfica de Colombia, 1963). https://www.sogeocol.edu.co/documentos/078_rasg_bio_abel_bravo.pdf

Céspedes Alemán, Francisco S. *La Educación en Panamá: panorama histórico y antología.* (Panamá: Imprenta Universitaria Biblioteca Cultural Panameña, 1981), pp. 28 and 43..

Coletta, Michela. *Decadent Modernity. Civilization and 'Latinidad' in Spanish America 1880–1920.* (Liverpool: Liverpool University Press, 2018).

Culiolis, Andrés. *500 años de Educación en Panamá. Análisis crítico-político.* (Madrid and Panamá: Editora Escolar, S.A. – Susaeta Ediciones, S.A., 1992.

Dávila Florez, Manuel. *Cartas de Instrucción Pública* (Panamá: Tipografía M. R. de la Torres, 1893).

El Aliento. Político, Noticioso y de Variedades. Serie I, N° 1–2 (Panamá: 15 January 1891–30 January 1891).

El Boletín Diocesano. Año I, Año IV. N° 10–11, 19–20, 89–92, 94, 96109 (Panamá: Diócesis de Panamá, Administración de la Secretaría del Obispado, 15 November 1893–15 December 1897).

El Sufragio: Órgano del directorio eleccionario de Panamá. N° 2–3, 9–10 (Panamá: Imprenta de M. R. de la Torre e Hijos, 30 May 1891–20 August 1891).

Hurtado, Manuel José. 'La profesión de maestro' in *La Educación en Panamá: panorama histórico y antología*, Céspedes Alemán, Francisco S., comp. (Panamá: Imprenta Universitaria Biblioteca Cultural Panameña, 1981).

———. 'Testamento', in Juan Antonio Susto, 'Manuel José Hurtado, fundador de la Instrucción Pública en el Istmo', *Revista Lotería* N° 55 (Panamá: Diciembre, 1945).

Kirkendall, Andrew J. 'Student Culture and Nation-State Formation' in *Beyond Imagined Communities. Reading and Writing the Nation in Nineteenth-Century Latin America.* John Charles Chasteen and Sara Castro-Klarén, eds. (Washington, D.C., Baltimore and London: Woodrow Wilson Center Press – The Johns Hopkins University Press, 2003), pp. 84–111.

Laird, Andrew and Nicola Miller, eds. *Antiquities and Classical Traditions in Latin America.* (Chichester: Wiley, 2018).

La Reseña Escolar: Órgano Oficial de la Secretaría de Instrucción Pública. Año 3. No 1–Año 4. No. 10. (Panamá: Tipografía Moderna, January 1907–October 1908).

La Reseña Escolar: Periódico oficial de Instrucción Pública. Tomo V, N° 48, 50, 54–56 (Panamá: Imprenta de Pacífico Vega, 10 April 1897–15 December 1897).

Londoño-Vega, Patricia. *Religion, Culture, And Society in Colombia. Medellín and Antioquia 1850–1930.* (Oxford: Oxford University Press, 2002).

Méndez Pereira, Octavio. *Historia de la instrucción pública en Panamá.* (Panamá, Editorial La Moderna, 1916).

Miller, Nicola. Keynote Speaker. 'Republics of Knowledge in Latin America' in *I Congreso de Historia, Antropología y Turismo Histórico-Cultural,* (Panamá: Universidad de Panamá, 2019).

Ministerio de Instrucción Pública. *Informe presentado al Congreso de la República en sus Ordinarias de 1888 por el Ministro de Instrucción Pública.* (Bogotá: Imprenta de la "Luz", 1888).

———. *Informe que el Ministro de Instrucción Pública presenta al Congreso de Colombia en sus sesiones de 1890.* (Bogotá: Imprenta de 'La Luz', 1890).

Moore, Barrington Jr. *Injustice. The Social Basis of Obedience and Revolt.* (New York: M. E. Sharpe Inc., 1978), pp. 17–23 and 440–445.

Paúl, José Telésforo. Bishop of Panama. *Carta Pastoral del Illmo. Sr. Dr. José Telésforo Paúl, Obispo de Panamá, al venerable clero y fieles de su diócesis.* N° 1. (Panamá: Imprenta del *Star and Herald*: Abril de 1876).

————. Bishop of Panama. *Carta Pastoral de José Telésforo Paúl al venerable clero y fieles de su diócesis.* (Panamá: Imprenta del *Star and Herald*, 1883).

Pérez, Manuel José. *Ensayos Morales, Políticos y Literarios.* (Panamá: Imprenta de M. R. de la Torre, 1888).

Revista del Asilo de Niñas. No. 22 Año 2. and No. 39 Año 3. (Panama: Imprenta de Samuel N. Ramos, 1 March 1892 and 1 July 1893).

Safford, Frank. *The Ideal of the Practical. Colombia's Struggle to Form a Technical Elite* (Austin and London: University of Texas Press, 1976).

Susto, José Antonio and Simón Eliet Simón. *La Vida y Obra de Manuel José Hurtado.* (Panamá: Talleres Gráficos, 1921).

CHAPTER 4

Conclusion

The discourse of some Panamanian liberals proposed the transformation of Colombian and Panamanian society following the precepts of positivism and cosmopolitan reason, which included scientific and technological development, a notion of progress which could be linked to inter-oceanic transit. But Panamanian intellectuals and the pedagogical elite did not limit their discussions or school programmes to spread and teach students the technical and intellectual skills necessary to acquire a career connected to the exploitation of Panama's geographic location. This book disagrees with the emphasis on the role of liberalism in Isthmian nation-building because this account overlooks the influence of other ideologies in Panamanian intellectual life. Although some of the existing bibliography observes the transformation of liberalism in Panama, these narratives describe this process as happening in a vacuum in the 1920s and 1930s as a result of disappointment with modernisation after the Canal was built, and also a desperate attempt to save liberalism from socialist movements.

To demonstrate its argument, the book applied Anderson's ideas on print-capitalism. This was an effective instrument to construct political, provincial or national consciousness leading to the development of a sense of belonging to an 'imagined community'. The book corroborates that in Colombia and Panama newspapers divulged information about events in different parts of the country. Projecting national news might have been the

© The Author(s) 2020   139
R. de la Guardia Wald, *Education, Conservatism, and the Rise of a
Pedagogical Elite in Colombian Panama*,
https://doi.org/10.1007/978-3-030-50046-7_4

most useful resource that the Colombian and Panamanian identity-builders might have had to define the national space in distant states or departments like Panama. Thus the press seems to have made Panamanians develop, at least partly, a Colombian identity. Anderson argues that news published in periodicals is ephemeral. Yet in Panama during the period studied, in spite of the brief existence of any particular periodical, other newspapers founded afterwards kept publishing the same or similar ideas. Furthermore, even when a particular story did not permeate national consciousness permanently, its sonority reverberated in the next publications about other events. Hence, it is possible to say that the success of print-capitalism in creating a cohesive collective mind frame depended on the daily ceremony of exposing the audience not to the same periodical, but to the same discourses of the writers and publishers, who attempted to preserve their discourse through explicit or implicit repetition of their message.

The verification of these arguments was illustrated, especially in Chap. 2. It offered a comprehensive view of the political alliance between the *Liberales Independientes* and Conservatives prior to Panamanian independence. These parties incorporated into their discourse of progress Rafael Núñez's interpretation of Spencerian positivism and Miguel Antonio Caro's conservative notions of morality. This was done, partly, for practical political purposes; however, as this work points out, there were already discursive and ideological similarities that brought them together. Both Núñez and Caro interpreted and adapted positivism and conservatism to the benefit of their political agenda. For instance, they were both strong critics of the *Liberales Radicales*' utilitarianism and both vouched for strong centralised leadership, but also shared common visions of how society and history should work. Núñez as a positivist accepted the idea that Colombia was in the destructive stage. In order to change this situation, social order and moral regeneration were needed to stop the chaos that *radicalismo* had caused. This idea was backed up by Caro. He maintained that society had lost its sense of morality. In his article, 'Historia y Filosofía', however, Caro sustained that this decline was necessary, because only out of a failed society could a new, better one emerge. After 1886, they both sustained that, in order to create a better political system, a moral renovation through the promotion of Catholic values was crucial. In theory, their political plan also included cross-party political tolerance and elevating the 'right to justice' over the 'right to liberty', or 'liberty within justice'. These three practices would bring a kind of social order that Núñez called *Paz Científica*. Once that condition was reached, the government would be able to produce policies for material and intellectual progress.

After identifying the philosophical pillars and the main political plans of *La Regeneración*, Chap. 2 presented the ways Panamanian and Colombian intellectuals and politicians were in contact with contemporary debates, absorbing and adapting conceptions to their view of local or national reality, especially the elements related to recovering of order, morality, or peace. This discourse also shows the way some Panamanian intellectuals and politicians envisioned their country's future and perceived moments of backwardness, 'crisis' and 'decadence' in opposition to epochs of 'progress' and modernity. It also claimed that bringing back conservative or traditional values and implementing scientific practices would help Colombia to modernise. Through this study it was possible to see how these practices were accepted or rejected in the Isthmus. The chapter shed light on the role of the Conservative and *Liberal Independiente* press in promoting Caro and Núñez's political programme. In this way, it examined the evolution of Panamanian newspapers' perception of *La Regeneración* between 1878 and 1903.

More specifically, Chap. 2 analysed the process of transformation of Panamanian liberalism and conservatism, in which different political factions adopted of the discourse of *La Regeneración* to constitute party identity. By studying *Liberal Independiente* and Conservative newspapers published in Panama, and how they embraced or rejected the *La Regeneración*, the book discloses a clear evolutionary pattern: initially Conservatives and many Liberals were suspicious of Núñez's plans; after 1880, some supporters, such as Pablo Arosemena, abandoned him; by 1885, Conservatives and *Liberales Independientes* were enthusiastic about political reform, while *Liberales Radicales* became ever more critical of the policies of *La Regeneración*, yet later on some of the latter introduced the concepts of *Paz Científica* in their discourse. Over time, however, it seems that many Isthmian newspaper writers became disillusioned with the lack of effective political reform. The Isthmus manifested scepticism regarding the capacity of the Colombian government to realise the alleged goals of *La Regeneración*. This distrust increased when, in 1891, the Conservative faction of the National Party split due to a dispute regarding the presidential candidacy of Marceliano Vélez, who ran against Núñez. This led to heated debates that compared Vélez to the government's vice-presidential candidate, Caro. However, even in the midst of these animosities, some Panamanian writers and newspapers continued to support the governing factions and called for reconciliation. Panamanian periodicals published during the three years before secession, nonetheless, showed a mixture of resignation and hope regarding the achievements of the political reform. On the one hand, some despaired because, in their language, the National and Conservative parties had become corrupted; on the other, the publications still hoped for social that they perceived had yet to begin in Colombia. Whether purposefully or not, it is perhaps remarkable that many Liberal newspapers called on politicians to establish peace and social order, adopting one of the key discursive expectations of *La Regeneración*. Paradoxically, then, the divulgation of news about the partisan disputes in Panama and the rest of Colombia may have exacerbated the sense of political division in the country, but, at the same time, it raised national awareness in a dichotomic manner: it promoted national consciousness as different regions of Colombia, including Panama, learned of events elsewhere in the country; in opposition to this, the information acquired also helped to form perceptions of different interests and generate discourses of provincial or political belonging and otherness.

Additionally, Chap. 2 studied how the Church, as well as professional and intellectual societies (*Sociedad de Medicina y Cirugía de Panama* and *Sociedad 'El Progreso del Istmo'*) divulged discourses of modernity and progress. It explored the Pastoral Letters of the Bishops of Panama. Also, it studied how the speeches of the Sociedad 'El Progreso del Istmo' to celebrate Panama's independence from Spain displayed proto-national sentiments and promoted the importance of education. The chapter looked at the writings of Panamanian scientists, especially medical doctors, who promoted the teaching of science and the professionalisation of scientific careers. Isthmian doctors founded associations to protect their trade, but also to exercise political pressure. They did this through their *Sociedad de Medicina y Cirugía de Panamá*. The chapter highlighted a detail to take into account: the main leaders of the medical association were conservatives or moderate liberals. More importantly, the chapter emphasised how there was a relation between the goals of the Church, the *Sociedad 'El Progreso del Istmo'* and The government of *La Regeneración*'s aims of achieving scientific as well as spiritual progress in Panama.

All these changes were contrasted with the arguments of Kosselleck and Miller shedding light upon how sensations of stagnation and crisis call for reform and regeneration. Based on the work of those authors, the book argued that political changes bring about new 'spaces of experience' that do not necessarily correspond to the desired experience: progress or modernity. The deferral of modernity produces reconfigurations of the plans for regeneration. The chapter, then, uncovered to our eyes the adaptability of conservatives and moderate liberals, which permitted to redesign discourses and imagine new 'horizons of expectations'.

The book analysed the structuring of the Panamanian educational system in the late nineteenth century. Chapter 3 argued that those groups involved in the configuration of education in Panama between 1878 and 1903, namely the Church, professionals, politicians, educators and intellectuals agreed on one point: the need to create a pedagogical elite. This elite was to be tasked with curating a curriculum and thus delineating the remit of public knowledge, as taught in Colombian and Isthmian schools. The aim was to design programmes of moral and practical education that would produce not only citizens with technical or scientific skills but also with an elevated sense of civic and ethnic nationalism through the teaching of national history and geography, the national religion (Catholicism) and the national language. Chapter 3 expounded how the notion of moral regeneration had an effect on the design of the curricula and assessment by members of a pedagogical elite. Based on the study of the concepts 'spaces of experience' and 'horizons of expectations' by Reinhart Kosselleck, and of the concepts of 'cosmopolitan reason' and 'projects of abjection' by Thomas Popkewitz, Chap. 3 commented on how the Enlightenment ideal of uniting humanity influenced Colombian and Panamanian educators' quest for fostering their particular notions of modern and civilised behaviour and values onto the population. Specifically, this book is about connecting their appropriation and adaptation of cosmopolitanism to the language used by conservative and conservatised-liberals in the education sectors located in the Isthmus of Panama between 1878 and 1903. This appropriation was part of a process of selective inclusion/exclusion required to form a solid and united human continuum: the provincial or the national collective. Following this idea, I investigated how the reconstruction of spaces of experience (or the past/present) compelled Panamanian conservatives and moderate liberals to imagine that religion or Christian morality, as well as science, were necessary to fulfil their expectations under their principles of cosmopolitanism. Within this frame, as Popkewitz states, pedagogues and students were conceived as agents of the process of civilising a society. Yet they had to be 'tamed' so that they could become adequate guides towards progress and not decline. For this reason, and drawing upon Pierre Bourdieu's propositions, Chap. 3 defended the statement that within the education system, the tamed agents became members of the pedagogical elite: ministers or secretaries of public instructions, directors of schools, teachers inspectors of public instruction and leading teachers. These were the ones who could save both education and society, but only if they followed the precepts of *La Regeneración*.

More specifically, using Bourdieu's concepts of social space, as well as Miller's discussion on intellectuals, the chapter discussed how at the beginning of *La Regeneración* it was mainly conservative and moderate-liberal individuals graduated from teachers' schools or from universities who eventually became members of the pedagogical elite. It was concluded that the acquisition of a professional degree made teachers and students in *escuelas normales* perceived that they had authority and, therefore, the duty and right to formulate and divulge their vision of the nation. Yet, to become part of the elite it was necessary to obtain a cultural capital that helped reproduce a language that stayed within the philosophical margins set up by other conservative and moderate liberal intellectuals and pedagogues, governmental authorities, professional associations and the Church. Demonstrating the possession of this capital facilitated permanence in the same social space or an entrance to new social spaces. It was a symbol that some pedagogues belonged the political, economic, social and intellectual elites. To present this with clarity, Chap. 3 particularly analysed the labour of Manuel José Hurtado, Nicolás Pacheco, Abel Bravo, Melchor Lasso de la Vega and Nicolás Victoria Jaén. Working on this helped to show how this high profile educators managed the education system and constructed networks, especially during *La Regeneración*. As such, this moment constituted the birth of a pedagogical elite.

Referring to the works by Burke and also of Franklin, Pereyra and Popkewitz on the selection and dissemination of the kinds of knowledge that were considered adequate for Colombian and Panamanian children, Chap. 3 unearthed the ways in which leading educators or education policy-makers selected desirable information. It argued that the imposition of particular visions and knowledges delimited how various sectors of the population received it. These observations seem adequate for the understanding of the behaviour of pedagogues in Colombian Panama, where the moral and scientific knowledges presented in schools were approved through a scrutiny framed within conceptualisations of progress and modernity; science and reasonability; instruction and education; and the nature of children and adolescent students of the positivists, conservatives and conservatised-liberals. It was argued that even when educators, intellectuals and religious men fomented the combination of practical, scientific and intellectual education, they gave prevalence to moral and religious knowledge to form local (Panamanian) and national (Colombian) identities.

With limited primary sources, Chap. 3 analysed some of the school dynamics to reflect the students' exposition and reactions to the curricula, course content and assessments. The objective was to show to what extent they absorbed the pedagogical elite's views on worthy moral, scientific and practical knowledge. It also provided a sketch on the effectiveness of teaching methods. In relation to this, Chap. 3 evaluated how the pedagogical elite tried to ensure a legacy for Catholicism, conservatism, moderate liberalism and positivism in Panama.

Going on from this, I sustain that many Isthmian statesmen, whether they were conservative or liberal, developed models of prosperity that surpassed 'transitism' and pure material or economic growth for their own personal benefit and that of their inner circle. Panamanian conservatism, moderate liberalism and positivism produced views of modernity that adjudicated importance to other ideals and interests: national culture (Spanish language and Catholicism), order and peace, and 'moral renovation'. This investigation does not disagree with the argument that during the nineteenth century many members of the Panamanian elites envisioned the future of Panama as a 'commercial emporium', sustained by the existence of an inter-oceanic waterway. But taking into account other religious, cultural, political, social and intellectual expectations is of utmost importance to understand Panamanian history. The book also questions that the formation of the Panamanian nation was not solely determined by the US after it consolidated its presence in the Isthmus. It shows that the Panamanian elites were not living in intellectual obscurity before the US intervened in the Panamanian Independence in 1903 and began to build the Panama Canal. On the contrary, they had developed their own imagination of Panama's future, modernity and methods of nation-building.

ANNEX 1

NUMBER OF STUDENTS URBAN AND ALTERNATING PRIMARY
SCHOOLS IN THE DEPARTMENT OF PANAMA IN 1894[1]

Province/Type of School	Panama	Colón	Coclé	Los Santos	Veraguas	Chiriquí	Total
Urban boys' schools	20	6	6	10	9	9	62
Urban girls' schools	15	4	6	9	5	5	44
Alternating schools	2			2			4
Rural boys' schools							No data
Rural girls' schools							No data

[1] Alejandro Motta, Inspector of Public Instruction of Panama (?), in *Informe que el Ministro de Instrucción Pública presenta al Congreso de Colombia en sus sesiones de 1894.* (Bogotá: Imprenta de la Luz, 1894), p. XIV. The author broke down the original statistics table of the inspector for the better understanding of current readers.

© The Author(s) 2020
R. de la Guardia Wald, *Education, Conservatism, and the Rise of a Pedagogical Elite in Colombian Panama*,
https://doi.org/10.1007/978-3-030-50046-7

Number of Qualified and Unqualified Teachers in Public Primary Schools in the Department of Panama 1894

Province/Type of Teacher	Panama	Colón	Coclé	Los Santos	Veraguas	Chiriquí	Total
Male teachers with qualification	6	1	4	4	1		16
Male teachers without qualification	19	8	3	7	8	9	54
Female teachers with a qualification	2	1					3
Female teachers without a qualification	15	2	6	11	5	6	45

Students that Graduated from Public Primary Schools by Province and Gender in the Department of Panama by 1894

Province/Gender	Panama	Colón	Coclé	Los Santos	Veraguas	Chiriquí	Total
Boys	938	237	149	177	221	205	1927
Girls	786	91	249	119	101	134	1480

AGE MARGINS OF PUBLIC PRIMARY SCHOOL STUDENTS BY PROVINCE IN THE DEPARTMENT OF PANAMA BY 1894

Province	Panama	Colón	Coclé	Los Santos	Veraguas	Chiriquí
Age	4–23	5–17	5–16	5–17	5–16	5–17

Enrolment and Attendance

Total number of students enrolled:	4624					
Attending schools:	3407					

ANNEX 2

List of Graduate Students of the *Escuela Normal de Varones* 1874–1884[1]

Name	Place of Origin	Qualification	Date Granted	Director
Nicolás Pacheco	Panama	Secondary School Teacher	31 May 1874	Oswald Wirsing
Alejandro Meléndez	Panama	Elementary School Teacher	7 July 1874	
Manuel C. Jurado	David	Elementary School Teacher	7 July 1874	
Benigno Andrión	Penonomé	Elementary School Teacher	3 October 1874	
José María Barranco	Panamá	Elementary School Teacher	21 March 1875	
Segismundo Jaramillo	Penonomé	Elementary School Teacher	21 March 1875	
Alejandro Amí Cervera	Portobelo	Elementary School Teacher	16 May 1875	
Simeón Conte	Penonomé	Elementary School Teacher	27 November 1876	
Aurelio Guardia	San Carlos	Elementary School Teacher	27 November 1876	
Carlos Guardia	San Carlos	Elementary School Teacher	27 November 1876	
Abelardo Herrera	Penonomé	Elementary School Teacher	27 November 1876	
Agustín Almengor	Los Santos	Elementary School Teacher	27 November 1876	
Eliézer Jaén	Penonomé	Elementary School Teacher	27 November 1876	
Salvador Jurado	David	Elementary School Teacher	27 November 1876	
Juan Ayarza	Portobelo	Elementary School Teacher	27 November 1876	
Nemesio Pérez	Comarca de Balboa, Panamá	Secondary School Teacher	28 February 1879	
Liberato Trujillo	Ocú	Secondary School Teacher	28 February 1879	
Miguel Alba	Las Tablas	Elementary School Teacher	28 February 1879	
Vianor Apolayo	Penonomé	Elementary School Teacher	28 February 1879	
Estanislao Batista	Panama	Elementary School Teacher	28 February 1879	
Manuel María Grimaldo	Penonomé	Elementary School Teacher	28 February 1879	
Francisco Henríquez	Los Santos	Elementary School Teacher	28 February 1879	
Juan M. Mejía	Panama	Elementary School Teacher	28 February 1879	
Tomás A. Noriega	San Miguel, Comarca de Balboa, Panama	Elementary School Teacher	28 February 1879	
Juan Aquiles Ponce	San Carlos	Elementary School Teacher	28 February 1879	
Jacinto Conte	Panamá	Elementary School Teacher	29 October 1880	
Aníbal Aizpuru	Panama	Elementary School Teacher	29 October 1880	

Name	Place	Role	Date
Hortensio Herrera	Panama	Elementary School Teacher	29 October 1880
Manuel M. Pimentel	Antón, Coclé	Elementary School Teacher	29 October 1880
Felipe Bocarando	Capira, Panama	Elementary School Teacher	16 February 1881
José de la R. Poveda	Guararé	Elementary School Teacher	16 February 1881
Marcelino Villalaz	Los Santos	Elementary School Teacher	16 February 1881
Julio A. Jaramillo	Chagres	Elementary School Teacher	16 February 1881
Isaac Fernández F.	Penonomé	Elementary School Teacher	16 February 1881
Nicolás Victoria Jaén	Aguadulce, Coclé	**High School Teacher**	17 February 1882
Pacífico **Tapia**	Aguadulce	**High School Teacher**	17 February 1882
Eliseo Martínez	Penonomé	**High School Teacher**	17 February 1882
Adelio Ramírez M.	Penonomé	Elementary School Teacher	17 February 1882
Wenceslao Guial	Chame	Elementary School Teacher	17 February 1882
José L. Castillo	Cruces	Elementary School Teacher	17 February 1882
José S. Llorent	Los Santos	Elementary School Teacher	17 February 1882
Ricardo Meléndez	Bohío Soldado	Elementary School Teacher	17 February 1882
Patricio Meneses	Panama	Elementary School Teacher	17 February 1882
Francisco Vásquez	Taboga, Panama	Elementary School Teacher	17 February 1882
Sebastián Sucre	Aguadulce	Elementary School Teacher	17 February 1882
Jaime Carles	Penonomé	Elementary School Teacher	26 February 1883
Raúl Pérez	Chepo	Elementary School Teacher	26 February 1883
Hortencio Sayas	Panama	Elementary School Teacher	26 February 1883
José F. Lara	Natá, Coclé	Elementary School Teacher	29 October 1883
Manuel M. Herrera	Penonomé	Elementary School Teacher	15 February 1884
Melchor Lasso de la Vega	Aguadulce	Elementary School Teacher	15 February 1884
César Fernández	Penonomé	Elementary School Teacher	15 February 1884
Benjamín Quintero	Taboga	Elementary School Teacher	15 February 1884
Alcides Sandoval	Taboga	Elementary School Teacher	15 February 1884
José M. Huertas	Pesé	Elementary School Teacher	10 February 1885

For cross-referencing surnames look at those in bold font in this Annex 2 and Annex 5

[1] Ernesto J. Castillero R. and Juan Antonio Susto. *Panameños Ilustres: El Maestro Don Nicolás Pacheco. Símbolo del Magisterio Nacional (1853–1924).* (Panamá: Imprenta Nacional, 1953), pp. 25–32.

ANNEX 3

THE CURRICULA, BOOKS AND TEACHERS OF THE COLEGIO BALBOA (LYCEUM AND PREPARATORY LEVELS)[1]

Lyceum Courses	Rector Abel Bravo; Vice-Rector Lorenzo Barraza	Teachers of Lyceum Courses	Textbooks
Arithmetic I		Lorenzo Barraza	Lavalle
Arithmetic II		Abel Bravo	
Castilian [i.e., Spanish] Grammar		Abel Bravo	Ortología y Analogía by Roa
Universal and Colombian Geography			Compendio de Geografía de Colombia and Compendio de Geografía Universal by Carlos Martínez Silva (Colombian)
Reading and Urbanity			Manual de urbanidad y buenas maneras by Manuel Antonio Carreño (Venezuelan)
Religion I		Presbítero Javier Junguito	Exposición Demostrada de la Doctrina Cristiana by Ilustrísimo Sr. Juan B. Ortíz (Colombian) and FH Schouppe
Religion II		Presbítero Javier Junguito	
Calligraphy		Daniel Salcedo	
Historia Patria [Fatherland History]			
Sacred History		Presbítero Javier Junguito	
Latin		Presbítero Eugenio Navarro	
Ideological Reading and Composition		Abel Bravo	

[1] Abel Bravo. *Informe del Colegio Balboa. República de Colombia – Departamento de Panamá – Colegio Balboa – Rectoría – Numero 8 – Panamá, Abril 24 de 1890, Informe que el Ministro de Instrucción Pública presenta al Congreso de Colombia en sus sesiones de 1890.* (Bogotá: Imprenta de 'La Luz', 1890), pp. 293 and 295.

Preparatory Courses	*Teachers of Preparatory Level Courses*
Geography	Manuel Valentín Bravo
Reading	Manuel Valentín Bravo
Calligraphy	Manuel Valentín Bravo
Religion	Presbítero Eugenio Navarro
Sacred History	Presbítero Eugenio Navarro
Arithmetic	
Castilian [i.e., Spanish] Grammar	

ANNEX 4

Report on the Trimestral Exams Called 'Sabatinos' (Sabbatical) Reviewed in the Colegio (Balboa) Between 1 October and 2 October of 1897[1]

Course	Student	Grade	Average
Castilian I [i.e., Spanish I]	Evaristo López	5	4
	Vicente Urueta	2	
	Elías Aizpuru	4	
Castilian II [i.e., Spanish II]			
Arithmetic I	Antonio Arias	3	4
	Evaristo López	3	3
	Maximiliano Vélez	2	
Arithmetic II	Juan Francisco Guardia	4	3
	Januario Illueca	3	
	Tomás Illueca	2	
Descriptive Geography	Eduardo Kwon	5	5
	Armodio Arias	5	
	Vicente Urueta	4	
English I	César Mendoza	5	5
	Manuel Castillo	5	
	Antonio Ocaña	5	
English II	Ismael Ortega	5	4
	Eladio Briceño	4	
	Januario Illueca	4	

[1] Esteban Terradas, Rector. 'Acta de los exámenes trimestrales denominados como 'Sabatinos' verificados en este Colegio entre el día 1 y 2 del presente mes de octubre' in Reseña Escolar. Periódico Oficial de Instrucción Pública. Tomo V. Número 54. (Panamá, 16 de octubre de 1897), pp. 824–825.

Subject	Name		
French I	Américo de la Guardia	5	5
	Tomás Paredes	5	
	Istmael Ortega	5	
French II	Ricardo Alfaro	5	5
	Francisco Márquez	5	
	Ricardo Ardila	4	
Latin I	Julián Sosa	3	3
	Eladio Briceño	4	
	Félix Palacios	3	
Latin II	Federico Ardila	4	4
	Ricardo Ardila	3	
	Francisco Márquez	4	
Religion I	Eduardo Guardia	4	3
	Rodolfo Arce	5	
	Franklin Ribera	1	
Religion II	Ricardo Ardila	5	5
	Francisco Márquez	4	
	Ricardo Alfaro	5	
Historia Patria [Fatherland History]	Américo Guardia	3	4
	Mario Preciado	5	
	Ismael Ortega	4	
Algebra	Julián Sosa	5	4
	Moisés de la Rosa	4	
	Franklin Ribera	3	
Philosophy	Moisés Polo	5	5
	Serafín Achurra	5	
	Moisés de la Rosa	5	
Accounting	Rodolfo Arce	5	4
	Ricardo Ardila	3	
	Ricardo Alfaro	4	

ANNEX 5

© The Author(s) 2020
R. de la Guardia Wald, *Education, Conservatism, and the Rise of a Pedagogical Elite in Colombian Panama*,
https://doi.org/10.1007/978-3-030-50046-7

ESCUELA NORMAL DE INSTITUTORAS: CURRICULA AND GRADES MONTHLY REPORTS OF SEPTEMBER, OCTOBER, AND NOVEMBER OF 1897[1]

Name	Month	Reading	Writing	Castilian [i.e., Spanish]	Arithmetic	Geometry	Geography of Colombia	Sacred History
1, Ayala,	Sep	5	5	5	5	4	5	5
Eusebia	Oct	4	5	3	5	5	5	5
	Nov	5	5	5	5	4	4	5
2. Alderete,	Sep	5	5	5	5	5	5	5
Josefina	Oct	5	5	5	5	5	5	5
	Nov	5	5	5	5	5	5	5
3. Arjona,	Sep	2	3	4	4	5	4	4
Inés	Oct	3	3	3	3	3	3	5
	Nov	3	4	4	3	4	5	5
4. Andrión,	Sep	4	5	4	2	3	4	5
Ines	Oct	3	5	5	4	5	5	5
	Nov	3	5	5	5	5	5	5
5. Arias,	Sep	5	5	5	5	5	5	5
Eudocia	Oct	5	5	5	5	5	5	5
	Nov	5	5	5	5	5	5	No grade
6. Begovich,	Sep	4	4	4	5	5	4	4
Isabel	Oct	3	4	3	5	5	3	5
	Nov	4	4	5	4	5	4	5
7. Benítez,	Sep	2	4	4	2	3	4	5
Clementina	Oct	3	4	4	3	4	4	5
	Nov	3	4	4	3	4	4	No grade
8. Barrera,	Sep	3	4	5	4	5	4	5
Guillermina	Oct	3	5	3	3	1	2	5
	Nov	2	5	4	3	5	4	No grade
9. Casís,	Sep	5	5	5	4	5	5	5
Tomasa	Oct	5	5	4	3	5	4	2
	Nov	5	5	5	5	5	5	No grade

[1] Based on: Matilde Rubiano C and Rosa H. Rubiano C. Escuela Normal de Institutoras. Registro Correspondiente al Mes de Septiembre *Reseña Escolar* Tomo V. No. 54, Panamá: 16 de octubre de 1897, pp. 822–823. Matilde Rubiano C and Rosa H. Rubiano C. Escuela Normal de Institutoras. Registro Correspondiente al Mes de Octubre, *Reseña Escolar.* Tomo V. No. 55, Panamá: 15 de noviembre de 1897, pp. 837–838. Matilde Rubiano C. and Rosa H. Rubiano C. Escuela Normal de Institutoras. Registro Correspondiente al Mes de Noviembre, *Reseña Escolar* Tomo V. No. 56, Panamá: 15 de diciembre de 1897, pp. 849–850. The final average per course was calculated by the author of this book.

Urbanity	Religion	Pedagogy	Physical Geography	Calisthenic	Drawing	Music and Singing	Liquidation	Average
5	5	5	5	4	5	–	4	
5	5	5	5	5	5	4	4	4
	5	5	5	5	5	5	4	
5	5	5	5	5	5	–	5	
5	5	5	5	5	5	5	5	5
	5	5	5	5	5	5	5	
2	5	4	2	5	5	–	3	
3	5	3	4	5	5	4	3	3
	5	4	5	5	5	5	4	
5	5	4	3	5	4	–	3	
5	5	5	5	5	5	3	4	3
	5	4	5	5	5	5	4	
5	5	5	5	5	5	–	5	
5	5	5	5	5	5	3	4	4
	5	5	5	5	5	4	4	
4	5	5	4	4	5	–	4	
5	5	4	5	4	5	4	4	4
	4	5	3	5	5	5	4	
5	5	5	5	4	4	–	3	
5	No grade	4	4	5	5	5	4	3
	4	5	3	5	5	4	4	
5	5	4	3	5	4	–	3	
5	4	3	2	5	5	4	3	3
	3	4	3	5	5	4	3	
5	5	5	5	4	5	–	4	
5	5	5	5	5	5	4	4	4
	5	5	5	5	5	5	5	

Name	Month	Reading	Writing	Castilian [i.e., Spanish]	Arithmetic	Geometry	Geography of Colombia	Sacred History
10. Conte,	Sep	1	3	4	2	2	4	4
Delia	Oct	2	3	5	2	1	3	5
	Nov	2	2	4	4	4	4	5
11. Díaz,	Sep	5	5	5	5	4	5	5
Zoraida	Oct	5	5	5	5	5	5	5
	Nov	5	5	5	5	5	5	5
12. De la	Sep	5	5	5	5	5	5	5
Guardia,	Oct	5	5	5	5	5	5	5
Elvira	Nov	5	5	5	5	5	5	No grade
13. Esquivel,	Sep	5	5	5	5	5	5	5
Martina	Oct	5	5	5	5	5	5	5
	Nov	5	5	5	5	5	5	5
14.	Sep	1	5	4	1	5	5	5
Escudero,	Oct	3	5	5	5	3	4	5
Luisa	Nov	3	4	5	5	5	4	5
15. Fábrega,	Sep	5	5	5	5	5	5	5
Sofía	Oct	5	5	5	5	5	5	5
	Nov	5	5	5	5	5	5	5
16. García,	Sep	5	5	5	5	5	5	5
Modesta	Oct	5	5	5	5	No grade	5	5
	Nov	5	5	5	5	5	5	5
17. Guardia,	Sep	5	5	5	5	5	5	5
Emma	Oct	5	5	5	5	5	5	5
	Nov	5	5	5	5	5	5	5
18. Herrera,	Sep	3	5	5	2	4	4	5
Isabel	Oct	5	5	5	4	4	4	5
	Nov	5	5	4	4	4	4	No grade
19. Icaza,	Sep	3	4	4	2	5	4	4
Arcelia	Oct	3	3	4	3	4	5	2
	Nov	3	4	4	5	4	5	No grade
20.	Sep	2	3	4	3	4	4	5
Méndez,	Oct	2	3	3	4	5	5	3
Mercedes								
	Nov	3	4	4	5	5	5	No grade
21. Ocaña,	Sep	3	5	4	2	4	3	4
Cármen	Oct	4	5	3	2	1	3	No grade
	Nov	4	5	4	4	4	4	3
22. Ponce,	Sep	4	4	5	2	3	3	5
Manuela	Oct	4	4	5	2	5	2	2
	Nov	4	4	5	4	4	5	No grade
23. Ponce,	Sep	5	5	5	5	2	4	5
Jilma	Oct	5	3	3	4	4	3	5
	Nov	5	5	5	5	5	5	5
24. Ponce,	Sep	3	4	4	1	3	5	5
Dolores	Oct	2	4	5	2	No grade	5	No grade
	Nov	4	4	5	4	4	5	5

Urbanity	Religion	Pedagogy	Physical Geography	Calisthenic	Drawing	Music and Singing	Liquidation	Average
5	5	4	2	4	3	–	3	
5	No grade	4	4	4	5	3	3	3
	3	4	3	5	5	3	3	
5	5	5	5	5	5	–	4	
5	5	5	5	5	5	4	4	4
	5	5	5	5	5	5	5	
5	5	5	5	4	4		4	
5	5	5	5	5	5	5	5	4
	5	5	5	5	5	5	5	
5	5	5	5	5	4		4	
5	5	5	5	5	5	5	5	4
	5	5	5	5	5	5	5	
3	5	5	5	5	5		4	
5	4	4	5	5	4	4	4	4
	5	5	5	5	5	4	4	
5	5	5	5	5	5		5	
5	5	5	5	5	5	5	5	5
	5	5	5	5	5	5	5	
5	5	5	5	5	5		5	
5	5	5	5	5	5	4	4	4
	5	5	5	5	5	5	5	
5	5	5	5	5	5		5	
5	5	5	5	5	5	5	5	5
	5	5	5	5	5	5	5	
2	5	5	4	5	4		4	
5	5	4	3	5	5	4	4	4
	5	5	3	5	5	5	4	
5	5	5	5	5	5		4	
4	5	4	4	5	4	3	4	4
	5	5	5	5	5	4	4	
5	4	3	3	5	5		3	
5	No grade	4	3	5	5	4	4	3
	3	4	3	5	5	5	4	
5	3	4	4	4	5		3	
5	No grade	4	4	5	5	3	3	3
	3	4	3	5	5	4	3	
2	4	4	3	4	4		3	
5	No grade	4	3	5	3	3	3	3
	5	5	3	5	4	4	4	
5	5	5	5	4	4		4	
5	No grade	4	3	5	5	3	4	4
	5	4	3	5	3	4	4	
3	5	4	3	4	4		3	
4	5	3	3	5	5	3	3	3
	5	4	3	5	4	5	4	

Name	Month	Reading	Writing	Castilian [i.e., Spanish]	Arithmetic	Geometry	Geography of Colombia	Sacred History
25. Ponce,	Sep	5	5	5	4	4	5	5
Holda	Oct	5	4	5	5	5	5	5
	Nov	5	5	5	5	5	5	5
26. Rethy,	Sep	3	4	5	4	4	4	5
Ofelina	Oct	3	4	2	2	No grade	3	4
	Nov	3	3	5	5	4	4	No grade
27. Solano,	Sep	1	4	5	3	3	4	5
Posidia	Oct	3	4	3	4	5	3	No grade
	Nov	4	4	5	3	5	5	5
28. Sucre,	Sep	4	5	5	1	1	5	5
Delfina	Oct	3	5	5	5	4	3	5
	Nov	4	5	5	3	4	5	No grade
29. Sucre,	Sep	2	3	5	1	1	3	No grade
Carlota	Oct	2	2	3	2	4	2	5
	Nov	3	3	4	3	4	3	No grade
30. Tejada,	Sep	3	No Grade	5	2	2	4	4
Helena	Oct	4	3	3	2	5	4	5
	Nov	4	3	5	4	4	5	5
31. Tapia,	Sep	2	3	5	3	3	4	4
Candelaria	Oct	4	4	3	2	5	2	4
	Nov	3	4	5	4	5	4	No grade
32. Tapia,	Sep	1	2	5	5	5	4	5
Rosaura	Oct	3	2	5	3	No grade	3	No grade
	Nov	3	2	5	5	4	4	5
33. Vásquez,	Sep	3	3	3	3	3	5	4
Rita	Oct	2	4	5	5	4	4	5
	Nov	3	4	5	4	4	4	5
Average all students per course		3.71	4.23	4.51	3.84	4.2	4.28	4.7

For cross-referencing surnames look at those in bold font in this Annex 5 and Annex 2.

Urbanity	Religion	Pedagogy	Physical Geography	Calisthenic	Drawing	Music and Singing	Liquidation	Average
5	5	5	5	4	5		4	
5	5	5	5	5	3	3	4	4
	5	5	5	5	4	3	4	
1	5	5	4	3	2		3	
3	4	4	3	5	4	3	3	3
	4	4	4	5	5	3	4	
3	4	4	4	5	5		4	
5	4	4	3	5	5	4	4	4
	4	3	3	5	5	3	4	
5	5	5	5	4	5		4	
5	5	5	5	5	5	3	4	4
	4	5	5	5	5	4	4	
5	5	3	2	3	4		2	
4	No grade	3	1	5	4	3	3	2
	4	3	2	5	4	4	3	
3	5	3	3	4	5		3	
3	2	4	3	5	5	4	3	3
	4	4	3	5	5	4	4	
2	5	5	5	4	4		4	
2	5	4	4	5	4	5	4	4
	3	4	5	5	4	5	4	
5	5	4	5	4	4		4	
4	5	5	4	5	4	4	3	3
	2	4	4	5	5	5	3	
5	3	4	2	5	4		3	
5	2	4	2	5	5	5	4	3
	4	3	2	5	5	5	4	
4.42	4.59	4.42	4.05	4.79	4.65	4.15	4.33	

INDEX[1]

A

Abel, Christopher, 18
Aguilera, Salomón Ponce, 127
Aguilera, Santos José, 76–78
Aizpuru, Rafael, 49
Alea Jacta Est, 58, 60
All-Girls School of Penonomé, 130
All-Men Elementary School of San Felipe, 114
All-Men School of Antón, 130
Alterity, 77
Anales de la Academia de Medicina de Medellín (Londoño-Vega), 67
Anderson, Benedict, 32, 33, 139, 140
Arango Jr., Ricardo, 11n28
Arango, Ricardo, 11, 11n28, 116, 133
Araujo, Simón, 73
Ardila, Julio, 68
Arosemena, Conrado, 70
Arosemena, Demetrio Blas, 11n28
Arosemena, Gaspar, 68, 70–74

Arosemena, Justo, 12, 41, 42, 50, 70, 81
Arosemena, Pablo, 52, 53, 70, 85, 112
Arrabal, 100

B

Balmes, Jaime, 20, 54
Beluche, Olmedo, 16
Boletín de la Sociedad de Medicina y Cirugía de Panamá (Bulletín of the Society of Medicine and Surgery of Panama), 75, 76, 78
Books, 124–125
Bourdieu, Pierre, 22, 26, 27, 111
Bravo, Abel, 11, 114–119, 123–125, 133, 134, 144
Bravo, Enrique, 115
Bravo, Valentín, 110, 112, 115, 123
Brothers of Saint Vincent de Paúl, 97
Burke, Peter, 28, 144

[1] Note: Page numbers followed by 'n' refer to notes.

© The Author(s) 2020
R. de la Guardia Wald, *Education, Conservatism, and the Rise of a Pedagogical Elite in Colombian Panama*,
https://doi.org/10.1007/978-3-030-50046-7

C

Caesar, Julius, 59
Caicedo, Rodolfo, 1, 3–5
Calvo, José E., 76
Camacho, Indalecio, 80
Camacho, José Domingo Ospina, 58
Caro, Miguel Antonio, 5, 7–9, 21, 42,
    55, 56, 59, 140, 141
    moral revolution of, 46–49
Casas Rojas, Jesús, 91–93, 103, 134
Casís, Tomás, 51n51, 55
Catechism, 95
Catholic Church, 62–66, 133
Catholicism, 8, 46, 47, 49, 60, 65, 91,
    99, 104, 124, 143, 145
Catholic views, on pedagogies and
    Isthmus's informal education
    practices, 94–101
Cervera, Dámaso, 52
Charlatanism, 75, 76
Children, 31
Church, 94, 112, 114, 123, 128, 134
Civic nationalism, 46
Civil War of 1876–1877, 111
Colegio del Istmo, 119
Colegio del Rosario, 118
Colombia, 1, 4, 7, 12, 41–44, 46, 48,
    51, 53, 55, 56, 59–65, 67, 70,
    74–76, 79, 87, 91–94, 96, 103,
    109, 110, 116, 118, 122–124,
    127, 133, 139–142
    historiography, 17
Colombian Panama, 100, 121, 144
    regeneración and *Paz Científica* in
    (1878–1903), 41–87
    Sociedad 'El Progreso del Istmo' (The
    Society Progress of the
    Ishtmus), 68–75
Colunje, Gil, 81
*Compagnie Universelle du Canal
    Inter-Oceanique* (Ossa), 68, 116
Comte, Auguste, 19, 44–45, 54

Congress of Republic of
    Colombia, 9, 91
Conservadores Históricos, 51, 59, 60
Conservadores Nacionales (National
    Conservatives), 8, 9
Conservatism, 4, 12, 35, 42, 43, 55,
    60, 87, 140, 141, 145
    history of, 17–21
Conservative Party, 9, 41,
    59, 60, 142
Constitución de Río Negro
    (Constitution of Río Negro),
    47, 48, 61
Conte, Simeón, 112
Correoso, Buenaventura,
    12, 17, 110
Cosmopolitanism, 5, 143
Cosmopolitan reason, 22–24, 143
Cultural capital, 26–28
Curricula, 121–123

D

Davis, Harold Eugene, 20, 21
De la Ossa, Jerónimo (Gerónimo
    Ossa), 68–71, 74
De la Ossa, José Francisco, 68
De la Torre, M. R., 50, 51, 51n51,
    55, 68, 81
De la Vega, Mélchor Lasso, 80, 144
De Obaldía, José, 50, 81
De Roux, Gustavo, 68
De Roux, Luis, 68, 78
De Roux, Rodolfo, 68
*Declaración del 4 de noviembre de
    1903'* (Declaration of 4
    November 1903), 53
Delpar, Helen, 17
Department of Panama, 99, 108
Diario de Cundinamarca, 41, 42
Díaz Espino, Ovidio, 15
Diocesis of Panama, 96

Dirección de Instrucción Pública
(Directorship of Public
Instruction), 9
Donghi, Halperín, 32
DuVal Jr., Miles, 15

E
Education, 5, 9, 11, 20, 23, 26–31,
67, 70, 71, 78, 79, 91–94,
102–104, 107–110, 113, 115,
116, 118, 120–122, 127,
143, 144
children's, 134
in construction of professional,
partisan and national
identities, 32–34
in countryside, 129–133
formal, 79
group, 27
history of, 21–22
informal, 94–101
moral, 102
in Panama, 24–26
practical, 102–104, 110
public, 110
quality of, 9
religious, 8, 114
secondary school, 29, 116
Egalitarian practical
education, 101–108
El Aliento, 55, 110
El Aspirante, 54
*El Boletín de la Sociedad de Mecidina y
Cirugía de Panamá*, 78, 79
El Boletín Diocesano (*The Diocesan
Bulletin*), 96, 97
El Colegio Balboa, 98, 115–118
books, 124–125
curricula, 121–123
grades, 94–108
teachers, 123–124

El Colegio de la Razón, 114
El Colegio del Istmo, 73
El Constitucional, 56, 58
El Derecho, 52
Electores, 7
El Fiscón Impertinente, 51, 56, 57
El Istmeño, 41–43
Elitists projects of abjections, 102–103
El Orden, 59
*El País creado por Wall Street. La
historia prohibida de Panamá y su
canal* (Díaz Espino), 15
El Precursor, 50, 51, 51n51, 129
El Sufragio, 51
Empiricism, 75, 76
Ensayos Morales, Políticos y Literarios
(Moral, Political and Literary
Essays), 81
Escogar, Federico, 100
Escuela Anexa del Colegio Balboa (the
Annexed School of the Colegio
Balboa), 99
Escuela de Ingeniería Civil y Militar de
Bogotá (Civil Engineering and
Military School of Bogotá),
115, 123
Escuela de Niñas de Santa Ana (the
Lady's School of Santa Ana), 99
Escuela de Señorita, 10
Escuela de Varones de Santa Ana (the
Boy's School of Santa Ana), 99
Escuela Normal de Institutoras
(All-Girls Teachers
School), 10, 110
grades, 126–129
Escuela Normal de Varones (All-men
Teachers' School), 100, 111–115,
119, 130
Estado soberanos (sovereign states), 6
Estados Unidos de Colombia
(United States of
Colombia), 6, 42, 65

Estudios Morales
El Hombre' (Moral Studies: Mankind), 101
Ethnic nationalism, 46
Exposición Colectiva del Epicospado Latino-Americano (The Collective Exposition of the Latin American Episcopate), 96
Externado de la Sagrada Familia, 99

F

Fábrega, Francisco, 11n28
Fernández, Adolfo, 52, 112
Feuilleut, Tomás Martín, 68, 81
Figueroa Navarro, Alfredo, 17
Flórez, Manuel Dávila, 51, 51n54
France, 19
Franklin, Barry M., 34, 122, 144
Freedom
legal, 48
legal *vs.* moral, 48
moral, 48

G

Gougnon, Tomás, 96
Grades
El Colegio Balboa, 125–126
Escuela Normal de Institutoras, 126–129
Guardia, Aurelio, 112
Guardia, Carlos, 112
Guerrero, Manuel Amador, 1, 68, 78, 80, 133

H

Habitus, 26–28, 111, 115
Hale, Charles, 19, 43
Hanseatism, telealogy of, 12–14
Henderson, James, 20
Herbart, Johann Friedrich, 22

Hermanas de la Caridad (Sisters of Charity), 100
Herran–Hay Treaty (1902), 9
Historia y Filosofía' (History and Philosophy) (Caro), 46, 59, 140
Históricos, 60, 62
Hobsbawm, Eric, 32, 34
Holy egoism, 74
Horizon of expectations, 126, 143
Hospital Santo Tomás, 78
Huertas, Estaban, 1
Humanity, 93, 94, 103, 134
Hurtado, Manuel José, 10, 109–112, 114, 144

I

Icaza, Julio, 76, 80
Identity, 31, 50, 67, 73, 85, 87, 126, 140, 141, 145
newspapers and education, in construction of professional, partisan and national identities, 32–34
Panamanian, 5, 12, 35
Independientes, 7, 11, 12
Informal education practices, in Isthmus, 94–101
Instituto Nacional, 116
Intellectuals, 1, 12, 18, 21, 22, 24, 25, 27, 29–33, 35, 41, 43, 51, 54, 56, 79, 81, 85, 87, 94, 96, 102, 109, 117, 118, 123, 124, 134, 139, 141–145
Internado de la Sagrada Familia, 99
Isthmus, 1, 5, 10–14, 49, 50, 52, 53, 55, 63, 65, 69, 70, 72, 74–76, 85, 141, 143
Catholic views on pedagogies, 94–101
Independientes, 52
informal education practices, 94–101

J

Jaén, Manuel, 100
Jaén, Nicolás Victoria, 80, 144
Jaén, Victoria, 11
Jorge, Spaniard Santos, 127
Junguito, Javier, 123
Junguito, Presbítero Javier, 123
*Junta Central Directiva de Enseñanza
    Catequista* (Directing Central
    Council for the Teaching of
    Catechism), 96, 97
Junta de Higiene (Hygene
    Council), 80
Junta Directiva, 97
Jurado, Manuel C., 112
Jurado, Salvador, 112

K

Kirkendall, Andrew J., 113
Knowledge, worth of, 28–29
Kosselleck, Reinhart, 23, 28, 142, 143

L

La Escuela de la Fe (the School of
    Faith), 99
La Instrucción Pública' (Jaén), 129
La Lectura Popular (The Popular
    Reading), 97
La Luz, 41, 42
La Probidad, 61
La profesión de maestro' ('The
    Teacher's Profession')
    (Hurtado), 110
La Reforma (Hale), 19
La Regeneración, 4, 6, 7, 10, 18, 22,
    29, 32, 33, 35, 42, 52, 53, 55,
    58, 59, 63, 76, 79, 91–135, 141,
    142, 144
    discourse and pedagogical debates
        during (1876–1903), 94–108

foundations of, 43–46
    in Panama, negotiation of, 49–62;
        positivist and Catholic
        discursive incorporations,
        50–55; promotion, 55–62
    in Panamanian Conservative and
        Liberal *Independiente*
        newspapers, promotion
        of, 55–62
    in Panamanian education after 1903,
        permanence of, 133–135
    in Panamian state-building, legacies
        of, 85–87
    in schools, 121–133
    Panamanian Conservative
        philosophy during, 81–85
Las Huérfanas de San José (the
    Orphans of Saint Joseph), 99
Las Huérfanas de Santo Tomás (the
    Orphans of Saint Thomas), 99
La Sociología' (Comte), 44–45
La Sociología' (Núñez), 57
Lasso de la Vega, Mélchor, 11, 110,
    113, 114, 119–120, 127, 133
Late nineteenth-century Colombian
    Panama, 1878–1903, 6–11
Latin America, 29
Lemaitre, Eduardo, 16
Lemm, Max, 127
Liberales Independientes (Independent
    Liberals), 4, 6, 35, 41, 44, 47, 48,
    50–52, 54, 56, 60, 70, 110, 112,
    114, 140, 141
Liberales Radicales (Radical Liberals),
    6, 7, 41–43, 47, 52, 59, 110, 141
Liberalism, 4, 5, 12, 13, 19, 35, 42,
    43, 47, 55, 63, 65, 120, 139,
    141, 145
    conservatised liberalism, 87
    transformation of, 50–55
Liberal Party, 6, 43–45, 47, 59, 110
Liberal Radicals, 42

Libertad Radical (Radical
  Freedom), 47, 48
Liberty within justice, 53, 105, 140
Licenciados-políticos, 29, 30
Littré, Émile, 84
Lo Invisible' (Núñez), 56–57
Londoño-Vega, 67
Longue durée approach, 15
Los Derechos y Deberes de los Pueblos
  (The Rights and Duties of the
  Peoples), 104
Los niños, según el evangelio'
  (Jean), 133

M
Mack, Gerstle, 15
Marroquín, José Manuel, 9
Martínez Delgado, Luis, 16
Martínez, Eliseo, 113
McCain, William D., 14
McCollough, David, 15, 15n42, 16
Médicos por Intuición' [('Doctors by
  Intuition'), 78
Meneses, Patricio, 100
Metaphysical politics, 19
Mill, John Stuart, 6, 44
Miller, Nicola, 24, 25, 29, 30,
  142, 144
Ministry of Public Instruction, 99
Modernisation, 24, 139
Modernity, 1, 3, 23, 28–31, 121, 135,
  141, 142, 144, 145
  in Panama, 24–26
  technocratic, 25, 26, 133
*Modernization in Colombia: The
  Laureano Gómez Years,
  1889–1965* (Henderson), 20
Moleschott, Jacob, 84
Morality, 44, 48, 49, 55, 57, 60, 67,
  79, 83, 92, 93, 95, 101,
  115–119, 122, 127, 128

Catholic, 46, 63
Christian, 62
  total, 45
Moral renovation, 53

N
Nacionales, 58, 60
Nation, 46, 56, 65, 69, 71, 79, 93,
  122, 123, 133
National identities, newspapers and
  education in, 32–34
Nationalism, 121
  civic, 46, 143
  Colombian, 75
  ethnic, 46, 143
  teleology of, 12–14
National Party, 57–60, 141, 142
Newspapers, 41, 42, 50–52,
  54, 139–142
  in construction of professional,
  partisan and national
  identities, 32–34
Niñas, Asilo de, 100
Núñez, Rafael, 5–8, 17, 21, 42–46,
  49–57, 59, 61, 66, 71, 120,
  140, 141
  moral revolution of, 46–49
Nuns of Charity of Saint Vincent de
  Paúl, 100

O
Organic Law of 1887, 118
Ortega, Gerardo, 68
Ospina, José Domingo, 8
Ossa, Géronimo, 68

P
Pacheco, Nicolás, 110, 112–115, 144
Panaama, Constitution of 1886, 91

Panama, 139–143, 145
  Colombian, 41–87
  Constitutions of 1886, 7, 8,
    10, 61, 63
  Constitution of 1863, 41, 42, 45,
    48, 61; Article 92, 42
  education in, 24–26
  historiography, 17
  late nineteenth-century
    Colombian, 6–11
  modernity in, 24–26
  *su independencia de España, su
    incorporación a la Gran
    Colombia, su separación de
    Colombia; el canal interoceánico*
    (Martínez Delgado), 16
Panama Canal, 3, 145
  teleology of, 14–16
Panamanian Coat of Arms, 86
*Panamá y Colombia: Metamorfosis de
  una Nación* (Universidad
  Nacional de Colombia), 17
Paredes, Blas, 11n28
Paris Commune, 105
Park, James W., 17
Partido Nacional (National
  Party), 7, 59
Partisan identities, newspapers and
  education in, 32–34
Pastoral Letters of the Bishops of
  Panama, 142
Patriotism, 74
Paúl, José Telésforo, 7, 63–66, 67n90,
  94–96, 114, 115, 120, 134
Paz Científica (Scientific Peace), 120,
  140, 141
  in Colombian Panama
    (1878–1903), 41–87
  sociology for, 43–46
Paz y Progreso' (Peace and Progress)
  (Caicedo), 1–4
Pedagogical elite, 5, 22, 29, 30, 32,
  35, 73, 80, 139, 143–145

  birth of, 108–120
  discourse, practices and work
    of, 113–120
  rise of, 91–135
Pedagogues, 29–31, 108, 109,
  111, 118
Peralta, José Alejandro, 96
Peralta, Jose Antonio, 98
Pereyra, Miguel, 122, 144
Pérez, Manuel José, 51, 63, 72,
  81–85, 94, 101–107
  moral paradoxes, 101–108
Pérez, Nemesio, 112
Pestalozzi, Johann Hienrich, 22
Political parties, 53, 55, 58, 59, 76
Ponce, Jacinto, 129–133
Pope Leo XIII, 96
Popkewitz, Thomas, 22, 23, 31, 34,
  95, 96, 106, 122, 143, 144
Porras, Belisario, 52
Posada-Carbó, Eduardo, 19, 20
Positivism, 19, 47, 49, 57, 85, 139,
  140, 145
  Spencerian, 140
Prácticas Sabatinas' (Sabbatical
  Exams), 125
Print-capitalism, 139, 140
Professional identities, newspapers and
  education in, 32–34
Progress, 1, 3, 5, 7, 24–26, 28,
  29, 31, 44, 49, 56, 57, 59,
  61, 65, 69–73, 77, 79, 81,
  82, 84, 85, 92, 93, 102,
  105, 108, 110, 114,
  120–122, 124, 126, 130,
  133, 135, 139–144
  cosmopolitan, 22–24
  economic, 72
  material, 72, 83, 84, 87
  moral, 45, 75, 76, 84, 87
  scientific and technological, 82
  spiritual, 82
Projects of abjection, 143

R

Radicalismo, 49, 140
Rafael Núñez and the Politics of
    Colombian Regionalism,
    1863–1886 (Park), 17
Rangel, José de J., 130
Reasonability, 4
Red Against Blue. The Liberal Party in
    Colombian Politics, 1863–1899
    (Delpar), 17
Reforma, 44
Regeneración, in Colombian Panama
    (1878–1903), 41–87
Regeneration, 91, 93, 120
Re-Inventing Modernity in Latin
    America. Intellectuals Imagine the
    Future (1900–1930) (Miller), 24
Religion of Humanity' (Comte), 44
Republicanism, 45
Reseña Escolar, 114, 119, 125,
    126, 128
Reverendos Padres Escolapios (the
    Order of Calasanz), 11
Revista del Asilo de Níñas, 100
Revolución Moral' ('Moral
    Revolution') (Núñez), 49
Right to justice, 140
Right to liberty, 140
Rosas, Juan Manuel, 32
Rubiano, Matilde, 128
Rubiano, Rosa H., 128

S

Sabatino' Exams, 125
Safford, Frank, 11n28, 20, 111
Salvation story of education, 102
Sanclemente, Manuel Antonio, 9
Santander, Francisco de Paúla, 110
Schools, 94, 95, 97–100, 102, 104,
    109–119, 121, 124, 126–132
    La Regeneración in, 121–133
Schools of Arts and Crafts, 103

Seminario Menor (Lower
    Seminary), 10
Simon, Saint, 19
Smith, Anthony, 32
Social space, 26–28, 111–113, 115,
    123, 126
Sociedad 'El Progreso del Istmo' (The
    Society Progress of the Ishtmus),
    63, 68–75, 142
Sociedad de Medicina y Cirugía de
    Panamá (Society of Medicine and
    Surgery of Panama), 63, 68,
    75–80, 142
Soler, Ricaurte, 17, 18
Spaces of experience, 143
Spain, 19
Spencer, Herbert, 6, 44

T

Tapia, Pacífico, 113
Teachers, 92, 93, 95, 103, 104,
    108–115, 118, 119, 121–126
Technocratic modernity, 25, 26
Teleology
    of Hanseatism, 12–14
    of nationalism, 12–14
    of Panama Canal, 14–16
    of transitism, 12–14
Thiers, Adolphe, 19
Torres, José Agustín, 100
Transitism, 14, 145
    teleology of, 12–14
Trujillo, Liberato, 112

U

United States, 5, 15
    imperialism in Panama, 5
    triumphalism, 14
Universidad Nacional de
    Colombia, 17
Utilitarianism, 49, 140

V

Valentín, Manuel, 115
Variedades (miscellanious local news), 96
Vásquez, Eugenio, 119–120
Vélez, Marceliano, 8, 58
Victoria Jaén, Nicolas, 110, 113, 129, 133, 134, 134n134
Villalaz, Nicanor, 85

Vincent de Paúl, Saint, 10, 94, 96
Vogt, Karl, 84

W

War of the Books, 111
War of the Thousand Days (1899–1902), 9, 61, 62, 80, 129
Wirsing, Oswald, 111, 112, 115